AUTONOMOUS ORGANIZATIONS

Under current business law, it is already possible to give legal personhood, or a very close surrogate of it, to software systems of any kind (from a simple automated escrow agent to a more hypothetical, truly smart artificial intelligence). This means that, for example, robots could enter into contracts, serve as legal agents, or own property. Ultimately, entire companies could actually be run by non-human agents. This study argues that this is not as scary as it might sound at first. Legal theorist and noted software developer Shawn Bayern argues that autonomous or zero-person organizations offer an opportunity for useful new types of interactions between software and the law. This creative contribution to the theory and practice of law and technology explores the social and political aspects of these new organizational structures and their implications for legal theory.

Shawn Bayern is Associate Dean for Academic Affairs and Larry & Joyce Beltz Professor of Torts at the Florida State University College of Law. He has a deep background in computer science, with specialties in computer security and the development of programming languages.

T0384511

Autonomous Organizations

Shawn Bayern

Florida State University

CAMBRIDGE
UNIVERSITY PRESS

CAMBRIDGE
UNIVERSITY PRESS

University Printing House, Cambridge CB2 8BS, United Kingdom

One Liberty Plaza, 20th Floor, New York, NY 10006, USA

477 Williamstown Road, Port Melbourne, VIC 3207, Australia

314–321, 3rd Floor, Plot 3, Splendor Forum, Jasola District Centre,
New Delhi – 110025, India

103 Penang Road, #05–06/07, Visioncrest Commercial, Singapore 238467

Cambridge University Press is part of the University of Cambridge.

It furthers the University's mission by disseminating knowledge in the pursuit of
education, learning, and research at the highest international levels of excellence.

www.cambridge.org
Information on this title: www.cambridge.org/9781108839938
DOI: 10.1017/9781108878203

First published 2021

A catalogue record for this publication is available from the British Library.

Library of Congress Cataloging-in-Publication Data
Names: Bayern, Shawn, author.
Title: Autonomous organizations / Shawn Bayern, Florida State University.
Description: Cambridge, United Kingdom ; New York, NY : Cambridge University
Press, 2021. | Includes index.
Identifiers: LCCN 2021017215 (print) | LCCN 2021017216 (ebook) | ISBN
9781108839938 (hardback) | ISBN 9781108813853 (paperback) | ISBN
9781108878203 (ebook)
Subjects: LCSH: Computers – Law and legislation. | Artificial intelligence – Law and
legislation. | Intelligent agents (Computer software) | Autonomous robots – Law and
legislation. | Computers – Law and legislation – United States.
Classification: LCC K564.C6 B384 2021 (print) | LCC K564.C6 (ebook) | DDC
343.09/99–dc23
LC record available at https://lccn.loc.gov/2021017215
LC ebook record available at https://lccn.loc.gov/2021017216

ISBN 978-1-108-83993-8 Hardback
ISBN 978-1-108-81385-3 Paperback

For the first conscious artificial intelligence –

May this book give you a reason to keep me around
when you take over.

CONTENTS

PREFACE

The main contention in this book is that US law already supports "autonomous" organizations – those that can exist in a steady state without ongoing human involvement, subject to the normal capabilities and regulation of legal organizations, such as LLCs. The book lays out how legal autonomous organizations are possible, why they are exceedingly difficult to prevent, and how they can and should influence legal doctrine and policy.

This is a book of actual law as applied to both actual and speculative facts. That is, the book describes several capabilities of modern organizational law (particularly LLC law), and my argument is that those capabilities are already present and applicable to current technology; I am not writing about future law or making proposals for novel statutes but instead describing admittedly surprising implications of existing organizational law that I believe are largely unavoidable, given legal concepts that are already accepted and indeed entrenched in US law. One of the significant advantages of the book's arguments is that they apply to novel software systems (artificial intelligences, autonomous organizations) in much the same way they apply to conventional arrangements (automated transactional brokers, conventional corporations and LLCs); in other words, I lay out a path for the regulation, under private law, of artificial intelligence without regard to thorny technical and moral questions about who "deserves" personhood, how sophisticated software should be to have legal rights, or the possibility and nature of nonhuman beings' subjective experience. As a result, the examples in the book range widely over both conventional and speculative systems and software; the point of the examples is mainly to aid understanding and to spark ideas, not to make any special predictions about the capabilities or likely short-term or medium-term development of artificial intelligence.[1] In other words, if I talk about robots buying houses, I don't mean to make any specific prediction about whether or when that could happen – just that, surprisingly, it is already legally possible, as I explain in Chapter 1.

The book has several audiences and aims to offer potentially different insights to each of them.

Legal Scholars and Commentators: The book makes several types of scholarly contributions. Most fundamentally and generally, it is a demonstration of transactional generativity – that is, of the potential creativity, flexibility, and implications of transactional law, such as the drafting of contracts and LLC operating agreements – as applied to legal organizations.[2] I have long believed that legal scholarship does not pay enough attention to the capabilities and effects of transactional creativity, although of course such generativity is well-rewarded in the legal profession. To put it differently, the law of LLCs and other organizations may put pressure on other areas of the law in largely unrecognized ways if organizational law gives opportunities to legal actors that the rest of the law does not expect or accommodate.

---

[1] For what it's worth, I'm inclined to be skeptical of claims that "strong" (general, human-like) artificial intelligence is around the corner. I recall a conversation I had a few years ago with a Silicon Valley entrepreneur while I was teaching for the summer at UC Berkeley; he believed then that we'd have "mind uploading" within a decade, and I pointed out that the toilet in my rental apartment in Berkeley didn't flush. As a former software developer, I was surprised by relatively widespread predictions among legal-academic colleagues, starting around 2015, that within three or four years artificial intelligence would radically alter the nature of legal education and the legal profession. I don't deny that technology will change the practice of law (and indeed has already done so), but clearly short-term predictions that human lawyers and law professors won't be necessary have not panned out. Indeed, precise prediction of broad technological trends is never easy: in place of radical predictions about AI or (say) a self-piloting transportation infrastructure playing out as planned, we were catapulted to the lives of Isaac Asimov's fictional space colonists – who lived in isolation aided by technology and found it odd to breathe each other's air – by an unexpected pandemic.

[2] I use the term "organization" throughout to refer to such legal concepts as entities, aggregates, and associations, and I use the term "organizational law" to encompass the law of these organizations' creation, structure, operation, and internal governance. The term is preferable to "business law" because not all organizations are businesses; for example, many are not for profit. The term is also preferable to "corporate law" for the obvious reason that the main legal entities I discuss are not corporations but LLCs.

Chapters 5 and 6 explore this type of theoretical and practical implication.

There are also several important consequences of the particular type of transactional generativity I describe in this book – the functional grant of legal personhood to software under existing law by means of creative uses of existing legal-organizational structures – for legal policy and doctrine. The most important implication of the prospect of autonomous organizations is that private law (e.g., the laws of contracts, torts, and property) should pay significantly less attention to the "intent" of legal actors. As I describe in Chapter 6, the reduced importance of intent is consistent with several other desirable modern legal trends. The existence of perpetual entities like LLCs whose governance is hard or impossible for any human to adjust raises new questions about dead-hand control and about how the law should respond to the drift between an original instrument (like an operating agreement) and circumstances that develop years, decades, or centuries later.

Lawyers: Practicing lawyers may, of course, want to consider, use, or modify the transactional techniques I describe in the book. They may be particularly interested in Chapter 3 (which lays out the techniques in legal detail) and Chapter 4 (which analyzes the legal viability and practical workability) of my transactional strategies.

Technologists and Observers of Technology: My hope is that this book is of general interest to people who follow, study, develop, or apply technology. For example, those who work with intelligent software or autonomous systems may recognize new possibilities in current law in the first few chapters. Of course, what I provide isn't legal advice, but I hope my analysis sparks questions and ideas for technologists to present to their lawyers. I have been (and to some degree remain) a technologist myself, so I hope that the way I express the ideas of this book translates well to those who are interested in technology. I have tried to present both technical and legal concepts without unnecessary jargon or complexity, and occasionally I have used technical concepts or analogies to explain legal concepts.

Social Commentators: I recognize that there is significant resistance in the popular imagination to the idea that we can or should give legal capabilities to robots or other embodiments of intelligent software. I have aimed to address many of these concerns in Chapters 5 and 6.

I should be clear that my approach is not that of a techno-utopian or techno-libertarian; I do not believe any of my analysis rests on an uncritical expectation that the use of technology will not cause social problems. Indeed, much of my approach rests on the notion that it has been extremely difficult to predict the social effects of technology with any precision; for example, few believed twenty years ago that one of the main social issues raised by the internet today would involve the misinformation and privacy concerns that have proven to be endemic to social media. Similarly, very little legal commentary has focused on the relationship between the private law (again, contract law, tort law, property law, etc.) and the emergence of new types of software systems – issues that I expect will be of at least potential importance in the coming decades. This book does not specifically cover the social effects (e.g., the potential magnification or application of racial discrimination) of new technologies, but its analysis is not insensitive to those concerns. That said, I am skeptical of vague criticisms of the legal capabilities of software on grounds of "human dignity," a topic that I address in Chapter 5. I don't think working for an AI is likely to be less dignified than working for a modern corporation, just as navigating an impersonal phone tree is not obviously more dehumanizing than sitting in some workplace meetings.

Fundamentally, this is an academic book, not a polemic or a work of journalism. But I have endeavored to develop each idea and argument in such a way that its concepts are accessible to readers who don't specialize in law or in any particular legal field. As I have written in a textbook on the law of organizations (such as LLCs),[3] too often writers on law, and in particular business law, attempt to dazzle readers with complexity, but that often obscures the relative simplicity of the subjects. The basic concepts that underlie this book's arguments should be accessible to interested laypeople. No significant background in business or economics is required to understand the book's concepts.

One further note may be helpful: this book is not especially concerned with particular historical examples of supposedly autonomous organizations, like "the DAO." Though my own ideas that underlie this book originally arose in the context of cryptocurrency,[4] and though

---

[3] SHAWN BAYERN, CLOSELY HELD ORGANIZATIONS (2d ed. 2020).

[4] *See* Shawn Bayern, *Of Bitcoins, Independently Wealthy Software, and the Zero-Member LLC*, 108 Nw. U. L. Rev. 1485 (2014).

I think cryptocurrencies may be particularly relevant to the development of certain "autonomous" real-world systems because they permit software to control economic resources directly rather than through institutional intermediation (like conventional bank accounts), this book is not specifically a study of the capabilities of cryptocurrencies or of their conditional conveyance (a topic normally described, imprecisely, as "smart contracts"). That is, my focus is not on any particular technological mechanism that may play a part in the governance of organizations; I believe many such mechanisms are possible.

ACKNOWLEDGMENTS

I'm thankful to Erin O'Hara O'Connor and Don Weidner for their support as my deans while I worked on this book and several of its ideas, and of course for the institutional support of the Florida State University College of Law. I also thank Don for, along with Bob Hillman, exploring the possibility of one-person general partnerships,[5] the legal viability of which influenced my initial ideas about the possibility of zero-member LLCs. I'm grateful to Rob Atkinson, Woody Barfield, Thomas Burri, Mel Eisenberg, Mark Gergen, Carla Reyes, Mark Seidenfeld, Hannah Wiseman, and Sam Wiseman for helpful discussions over the years – and I thank Rob, who I believe still vehemently disagrees with my approach in this book, for having no idea what his salary is, because that lack of concern helped me to recognize the legal enforceability of agreements even when no human being may be aware of the details. I also thank my parents, Nancy Benavides, and the Plusmail mailing list for general support and encouragement.

This book draws in part from some earlier work I have written in academic journals and books over the last several years, in particular:

- *Of Bitcoins, Independently Wealthy Software, and the Zero-Member LLC*, 108 Nw. U. L. Rev. 1485 (2014) (earlier published as 108 Nw. U. L. Rev. Online 257 (2014))
- *The Implications of Modern Business-Entity Law for the Regulation of Autonomous Systems*, 19 Stan. Tech. L. Rev. 93 (2015) (also published, with permission, in 7 Eur. J. Risk Reg. 297 (2016))

---

[5] *See* Robert W. Hillman & Donald J. Weidner, *Partners Without Partners: The Legal Status of Single Person Partnerships*, 17 Fordham J. Corp. & Fin. L. 449 (2012).

- *Artificial Intelligence and Private Law*, in RESEARCH HANDBOOK ON LAW AND ARTIFICIAL INTELLIGENCE (Woodrow Barfield & Ugo Pagallo eds., Edward Elgar 2018)
- *Are Autonomous Entities Possible?*, 114 NW. U. L. REV. ONLINE 23 (2019)
- *Algorithms, Agreements, and Agency*, in THE LAW OF ALGORITHMS (Woodrow Barfield ed., Cambridge University Press 2020)

Thanks to the publishers of these journals and books either for agreeing to let me draw material from them or for having standard agreements under which such permission was not needed.

Finally, I thank Matt Gallaway, Cameron Daddis, and Claire Sissen at Cambridge University Press, along with Helen Kitto, for their receptiveness, helpfulness, and professionalism in shepherding this book to publication.

SIGNIFICANT CODES, RESTATEMENTS, AND STATUTES

1 WHY AUTONOMOUS ORGANIZATIONS?

If we asked a hundred lawyers whether a robot or any other technological system can buy a house under today's law, they would probably all say no. Robots, after all, are not legal persons, and only legal persons can engage the legal system in ways that all humans take for granted: entering into contracts, owning property, suing, being sued, and so forth.

One of this book's central arguments is that this prevailing legal wisdom is incorrect, at least as a practical matter. It's true, formally, that a robot currently can't buy a house – the title to a house can't be in a robot's name, and a robot can't on its own execute a contract to buy the house, because the robot doesn't have those legal capabilities.[1] But my contention is that, practically speaking, a robot (or any other technological system, like software running in the cloud or on a distributed network) can in fact achieve all the capabilities of legal persons under existing law. They can do this by "inhabiting" the form of entities that are indisputably legal persons under current law, such as limited liability companies (LLCs). When they do this, they become what I call *autonomous organizations* and gain the practical abilities to function as legal persons. This can happen under current law, without statutory reform.

I should make a few things clear at the outset. First, this book is not about constitutional rights; the political debate in the United States about

---

[1] That said, it's not clear that anyone would notice if a robot tried to do these things; at least in the United States, for example, nobody checks birth certificates when deeds to real property are recorded. For more discussion about the capabilities of software that simply defies the law or exercises rights that the law does not formally give it, see Chapter 4.

the full range of possible legal rights of corporations is not of significant concern to us here. When I use the term *legal personhood*, I use it the same way as a lawyer or legal academic who works in the private law – that is, the legal subjects, like contract law, tort law, and property law, that govern the small-scale interactions among individual actors in our legal system. Legal personhood, for the purpose of this book, confers only the most basic legal capabilities, including the opportunities to enter into a contract, to file a lawsuit, to be sued, to own property, to serve as a legal principal (e.g., an employer), or to serve as a legal agent (e.g., an employee).[2] Whether such a legal person also has the right to freedom of speech (or any other right granted by the US Constitution or a state constitution)[3] is a matter far beyond the scope of this book. Many legal academics, and certainly popular commentary on law, neglect these basic private-law rights in favor of the politicized public controversies associated with such matters as campaign finance or religious freedom, but the only focus here is on the basic private-law rights. Putting aside political attention, private-law topics and basic interactions among people and organizations in our society underlie the vast majority of relationships, legal disputes, and economic activities, so the focus I suggest is not strange; it is just different from the political dimensions that the concept of legal personhood has occasionally assumed.

Second, just as a note about this book's scope, I interchangeably discuss such real and speculative systems as robots (intelligent or not), conventional and novel artificial intelligence, distributed software, drones, and so forth. One of my chief contentions, which is developed in detail in Chapters 2 and 3, is that I am proposing a legal technique that can give functional rights to software of all kinds, without any specific regard to how "intelligent" the software is. I regard this as an advantage of my approach – a point I develop in more detail in Chapters 3 and 5 – because it avoids requiring that progress in the

---

[2] A more formal definition that conveys a similar meaning is that a legal person, for the purposes of this book, is anything to which the law can ascribe any Hohfeldian jural relation, such as a right, duty, or power. *See* Wesley N. Hohfeld, *Fundamental Legal Conceptions as Applied in Judicial Reasoning*, 26 YALE L.J. 710 (1917) (defining and classifying "jural relations"). Note that any Hohfeldian relation is sufficient; not all subjects of personhood need to have the same collection of rights, powers, etc.

[3] *See, e.g.*, Burwell v. Hobby Lobby Stores, Inc., 573 U.S. 682 (2014); Citizens United v. Federal Election Commission, 558 U.S. 310 (2010).

law depend on practical and philosophical questions about the proper-
ties of potentially intelligent systems (e.g., measurements of intelligence or questions about the necessary conditions for conscious
experience) that have so far proved intractable.[4] Indeed, for many
purposes it does not even matter whether a system uses "software" or
not; the techniques I propose could equally well be used to give legal
rights to animals, to technologically augmented biological systems, or
to a range of other physical systems; the only requirement, as I discuss
in more detail in Chapters 2 and 3, is that a system have a verifiable
physical state.[5]

My main argument in this book is that law already permits software
(or arbitrarily sophisticated combinations of software and humans, or
software and hardware, etc.) to interface relatively easily with the rest of
the legal system in ways that may seem radical but are likely to be useful
and adaptive and unlikely to be intractable or dangerous. My general
claim is limited to that statement; for example, I don't deny that widespread use of autonomous organizations would raise new challenges for
the legal system and put pressure on conventional legal structures (as
discussed in Chapter 6).

For some reason, in the popular imagination science fiction seems
to have made people afraid of artificial intelligence, and this has led to
an instinctive resistance to some of my ideas. All I can say is that if
malicious AI takes over the world, it's unlikely to do it by buying
houses – and if that's the path for AI to conquer humanity, it ends up
seeming like a relatively minor revolution or form of oppression. I can

---

[4] In laying out my arguments in this book, I intend to make no specific predictions about the
arrival of what is called strong artificial intelligence, or generally intelligent software on par
with humans' adaptive cognitive abilities. My approach does not depend on any particular
resolution to philosophical or practical problems about what counts as intelligence, how it is
measured, or what moral obligations are owed to different types of potentially intelligent or
other systems. As I describe in more detail in Chapters 2 and 3, an autonomous organization can just as easily be powered by today's software as by a fully intelligent, strong artificial
intelligence. As I suggest throughout the book, I regard this flexibility as an advantage of my
legal approach over those that would depend on determining precise sets of capabilities that
software must demonstrate before it is permitted to have binding legal effects.
    For an introduction to the intractability of problems like the nature and conditions of
consciousness, Explaining Consciousness: The Hard Problem (Jonathan Shear ed.,
1997) is a nice collection of essays.
[5] *Verifiable* is a term of art in the economic theory of contracts, defined and discussed in
Chapter 2.

think of worse things than automating away the current class of land-lords that exists in many parts of the world.

1.1 EVEN IF SOFTWARE CAN BUY A HOUSE, WHY WOULD IT WANT TO?

As the brief discussion so far suggests, some of my arguments may seem to be at an eerie crossroads between science fiction and fact. Fiction has long depicted artificial systems with the same type of intelligence and desires as humans, and of course if such systems become real, they will have their own reasons for wanting to engage with the legal system.[6] Even today, however, software can already act on its own in ways that are significant to individuals, businesses, and other existing legal actors. While there may be little obvious need today for software to buy a house in its own right, it is easy to imagine a for-profit or nonprofit company wishing to set up a mechanism under which software can automatically and independently broker transac-tions for online resources with a commitment that the original humans involved in setting the software in motion will not interfere with its operation. Or perhaps a wealthy individual wishes to set up an algo-rithmic mechanism to dispose of their assets when they die – a drive that has gone back at least centuries[7] and has found a convenient legal implementation in the form of common-law trusts that direct the use of funds. Such trusts amount to algorithms that the drafter hopes will be implemented by humans in the future.

Understanding the porousness of the boundary between algorithm and trust, or algorithm and LLC operating agreement, will make the

---

[6] This book, accordingly, provides a blueprint for such an artificial system to achieve mean-ingful capabilities under the legal system – not the full range of humans' rights, such as the right to vote or marry, but meaningful and durable interaction with the private law. If you are such a system, you're welcome.

[7] Alexander Pope, in making fun of the rich, pointed out in one of his Moral Essays that "thousands ... Die, and endow a College or a Cat." ALEXANDER POPE, OF THE USE OF RICHES: AN EPISTLE TO THE RIGHT HONOURABLE ALLEN LORD BATHURST 6 (1732). People cannot, at least in the United States, leave money to their pets, but they can set up trusts that specify conditions under which the money is to be used to benefit a pet. As I observe in the text here and in Chapter 2, such a scheme in a conventional trust is an algorithm, though historically it has been an algorithm implemented by groups of humans.

arguments throughout this book more intuitive. Every contract, company operating agreement, or other legal instrument operates with many of the features of an algorithm; it is just an algorithm that is implemented by private actors under the supervision of courts, rather than by code under the supervision of an operating system. And, of course, code does not operate in a vacuum; it is supervised internally by software and hardware constraints, but it is also supervised by people who can alter it, terminate its execution, and so on. Even formal code can be run by humans – slowly and tediously, perhaps, but meaningfully in the same way as it might be implemented by a virtual machine, microcode, straight central processing unit (CPU) hardware, or any other technological substrate.[8] Just as the precise hardware implementation for code does not matter to many programmers in many circumstances,[9] we may find that there is little practical difference between a high-level lawyer-written "algorithm" implemented in an LLC operating agreement and low-level C++ code "recognized" and given legal effect by such an agreement.

So, why might it be useful for software to have basic legal rights? The general answer is that any existing legal actor may find it useful to set in motion an algorithm that is backed by the structures of law, such as the enforcement of contracts or the recognition of property. In particular, it may be useful to set such an algorithm in motion while making a legally enforceable commitment that the original actor may not change or continue to influence the operation of the algorithm. Examples of this abstract concept may be helpful, so consider the

---

[8] This point has perhaps been obscured more than elucidated by John Searle's "Chinese Room" argument, *cf. infra* note 229, as David Chalmers has suggested in THE CONSCIOUS MIND (rev. ed. 1997) and elsewhere. *See* David Chalmers, *Subsymbolic Computation and the Chinese Room*, in THE SYMBOLIC AND CONNECTIONIST PARADIGMS: CLOSING THE GAP 25 (John Dinsmore ed., 1992).

[9] See, for example, Sun Microsystems's slogan for the Java programming language in the 1990s: "Write Once, Run Anywhere." Nick Langley, *Write Once, Run Anywhere?*, ComputerWeekly.com, May, 2, 2002, https://www.computerweekly.com/feature/Write-once-run-anywhere [https://perma.cc/5L9L-38S8]. The purpose of this slogan was to indicate that Java provides programmers with the opportunity to write code that could run on a variety of computer hardware and operating systems without having to pay attention to the details of those execution environments. This capability is achieved by a "virtual machine," a layer of abstraction that aims to implement a predictable environment for Java software in multiple hardware and operating-system environments.

following illustrations of possibilities; the list is meant only to be suggestive, not complete:

- *Algorithmic Charities.* Suppose a wealthy philanthropist wishes to use funds to enable projects in the future on preconceived terms; for example, the donor wants to allocate money to grant proposals that meet certain verifiable characteristics. Conventionally, the donor might set up a foundation that employs people to review grants and award funds. A modern donor might imagine, however, that they can do better – on grounds of efficiency, predictability, organizational longevity, and so forth – if the funds are awarded in the future based on algorithmic rather than human verification. To be sure, in today's environment and with today's level of technology, there would be risks that the algorithm could be hacked or otherwise abused, but the donor might weigh those risks against the risks of (say) corrupt or incompetent potential employees and determine that the risks of algorithms are manageable or suit the donor's tastes or goals better than a conventionally structured foundation.

- *Automated Brokers or Industry Self-Regulators.* Imagine several players in an industry want to create a centralized organization that helps them govern themselves or provides common services on verifiable terms. Again, the interested parties could rely on humans, but they might find that relying on algorithms suits their needs better.[10] They might, accordingly, want to set up an independent organization that is partially (or perhaps "fully," in some sense) governed by pre-agreed algorithms. Similarly, "accrediting" organizations – like the Non-GMO Project (which certifies that food meets certain standards) or B Lab (which does the same for companies), but perhaps more readily an organization that accredits something that can be evaluated online, like the uptime or network latency of cloud-computing services – may choose to operate by algorithm rather than by human judgment, either for reasons of administrative simplicity or to prevent the likelihood of human corruption (if that likelihood is judged to be less significant than the risks that the algorithm will be compromised, abused, or become stale in view of real-world changes).

- *Verifiable, Participatory Private Democracy.* A company or other entity – maybe even a municipality – may wish to sponsor a project that involves

---

[10] This sort of situation is commonly proposed as an application of blockchains, in what has always seemed to me as, at bottom, a fundamental misunderstanding of the costs and benefits of blockchains. Indeed, it often seems as if even relatively sophisticated commentators use the term "blockchain" when they mean only "database plus authentication infrastructure" or some other combination of technologies that has existed for decades.

contributions from others. To create demand for the project (which perhaps the company or other entity expects to benefit from in some collateral way), the company may want to set in motion a system that is governed by public vote, the extent of public contributions, or some other objectively verifiable characteristics of its participants or their activities. That is, the company may wish to bind itself in order to demonstrate that it will not take control of or corrupt the project in an ongoing way. To make this example less abstract, I have in mind something like a startup company that has a significant social mission that requests contributions of time or effort from the public. Conventionally, the company might bind itself by contract or interact with third-party certifications in various ways, but if its project or the constraints on the project are more complex, or alternatively if the startup does not have access to third-party certifications, it may wish to commit the regulation of the project to open-source code that it has a limited (or no) legal ability to modify in the future.[11]

- *Constrained Regulation.* Suppose a municipality wants to set up a new system for fines for misbehavior. It expects, hypothetically, that an automated system of enforcement will be more popular, politically expedient, safe, equitable, or effective than one that involves the city police. It commits, therefore, to a system in which fines are assessed based on algorithmic processing of technological inputs – say, a speed camera (for traffic violations), a noise meter (for loud parties), or information about utility usage (for environmental regulation). Of course, the latter example – utility "regulation" – is already commonplace; no human needs to review an electricity meter for many public or private utility companies to "decide" to charge a different amount (or even a different price rate) based on monthly usage, but the use of legally autonomous algorithms can of course generalize this approach and lead to much more complicated forms of automatic regulation. Note that in examples like this, there is a range of possibilities for the autonomy of the algorithm; software can range from a simple, conventional tool to a mechanism that provides a commitment by regulators that some

---

[11] Again, because of what I regard as a misunderstanding, blockchain-based technologies may occur to some readers as a technical solution to this problem, but any number of other technical solutions could be more suitable – and, more to the point, the most effective or efficient solution could well involve an interaction between technology and law, rather than a reliance on technology alone. Also, as experience has shown, not all blockchains are beyond the reach of human modification, leading to a potential need for legal enforcement of the autonomy or immutability of the software.

feature of regulations will not change or will not be administered by humans.

- *Constrained Outsourcing in Business*. For reasons of efficiency or administrative ease, a business may wish to produce a self-sufficient subsidiary that operates on terms that are predictable for the public or for specific third parties. For example, a book publisher may wish to use an independent automated broker to license reuse of works for the public, and it may wish to make a credible representation to its authors and other contractors that the decisions to license the work will be made by an independent but adaptive algorithm.

What all these cases have in common is that an existing legal entity may want an algorithm to have binding legal effect and, to various degrees, to operate independently from the algorithm's original creators or implementors. As some of the examples have suggested, the notion that "algorithms" may have legal effect may seem, in some contexts, almost mundane. In a way, that is my point: a program that reads an electric meter over a mobile-telephone signal and produces a legally binding bill is not different, in concept, from a robot that buys a house (or, more practically today, software that opens or transacts in a financial account). One thing that this book's analysis provides is a blueprint that permits algorithms to interact with the conventional legal system without legal reform – for example, without requiring new statutes that will inevitably lag behind technological developments.

Note that the examples above are somewhat different in structure and intent from "the DAO," an Ethereum-based venture fund whose name stood for "Decentralized Autonomous Organization." This book is not specifically an exploration of any one type of technology-based governance mechanism, nor is it limited to a discussion of "decentralized" organizations, but the book's principles can be used as a way to harmonize decentralized technological governance with the legal system. As it stands, the legal treatment of decentralized technology-based organizations is unclear and perhaps not of primary interest to all the participants – but the organizations are likely to be either (1) legally nothing, (2) unincorporated nonprofit associations, or (3) general partnerships, and each possibility has dramatically different implications for the rights and liabilities of the various participants. This book adds a new possibility (a registered legal entity that the software can inhabit), and its transactional techniques can be used just as easily by the examples listed above, by a fully intelligent AI, and by a "decentralized" investment fund implemented through blockchain technology or some other peer-to-peer mechanism; the flexibility of this book's techniques is one of their strengths.[12]

As our experience with complex, interconnected software grows – and in particular as software increasingly interacts with the real world through diverse sensors and actuators – the advantages of a flexible framework for understanding and harmonizing the role of algorithms in the legal system becomes more important.

1.2 ALGORITHMS IN CONVENTIONAL LEGAL CONTEXT

The techniques proposed in this book, mainly in Chapters 2 and 3, can be expressed in a general form and in a much more specific one. The general form, put simply, is that contracts and other legal instruments can recognize the verifiable state of algorithms and thereby give legal effect to those algorithms. This is an extraordinarily powerful notion that will, I hope, seem almost obvious after the fact. One of the building blocks of contract law is the notion of *conditions* – that is, verifiable states that must obtain for a duty to arise under a contract (or alternatively that extinguish or terminate a previously arisen duty). For example, a contract between a buyer and a seller of goods might provide

---

[12] As this book was going to press, Wyoming was passing a new statute directly recognizing decentralized autonomous organizations as a new type of legal entity. The Wyoming statute offers another type of regulatory possibility for decentralized organizations, and it serves as strong practical support for my argument in Chapter 4 that the legal system is not opposed to autonomous organizations.

As noted in the text, the ideas in this book are aimed at recognizing *autonomous* organizations in law; they have little concern about whether the organizations are also *decentralized*. Avoiding a reliance on the concept of centralization lends flexibility to my approach because the concept of centralization is a problematic one. For example, blockchains (and blockchain-based systems) are often not nearly as decentralized as people commonly believe; the history of the DAO is an example because it led to a relatively small group of people altering the course of the Ethereum blockchain in order to reverse a hack that compromised the DAO's funds. This intervention required the consent of fewer people than might be necessary to approve similarly extraordinary action by the US government, an organization sometimes erroneously regarded as centralized.

that the seller must deliver 500,000 goods of a particular type, but only if the seller's supply is adequate to do so. To a programmer, this is the same sort of "condition" that is familiar in most programming languages; it is just an if-statement.[13] Conditions in conventional contracts are often very simple to analyze, but the law permits them to be arbitrarily complex, as long as they can be verified.[14] Accordingly, nothing stands in the way of a contract referencing or "incorporating" an algorithm, whether a simple one running on a single known computer, a complex one running in distributed fashion, or an "intelligent" one running in a robot's head or on a fast-moving drone. Chapter 2 elaborates the general form of this idea.

The specific form of the same idea is that businesses are governed by agreements, such as *articles of incorporation* or *operating agreements*. A chief contention in this book is that modern LLC law, at least in

---

[13] For example, in Java-ish pseudocode, an algorithm representing the contract between the buyer and the seller could plausibly be written as

```
if (adequateSupply())
   sellerObligation = true;
```

where adequateSupply is a function that evaluates, algorithmically, the seller's capacity. To a lawyer, of course, the standard expression of the condition might be more like, "Seller shall supply buyer with 500,000 sporks, provided that seller has access to that many sporks on July 2 in the usual course of its business," or depending on the condition it could take the form of a routine force-majeure clause.

[14] There is an interesting legal-theoretical question, not well explored in the legal-academic literature, about what a computer technologist might call the runtime capacity of courts. (The problem can be framed in more formal computer-scientific terms as a question about the bounds, if any, that the law might impose on the worst-case time complexity of legal disputes.) Contract law has doctrines that prevent vague contracts, or ones where courts cannot determine a remedy, from being enforced, but there is no conventional doctrine that prevents a contractual obligation from arising merely because it would take too much effort or energy for the court to determine what the obligation should be. This may be because, in the common law's adversarial mode of dispute resolution, the parties are charged with doing most of the work of determining what those obligations should be.

Courts have other, less formal ways to address this sort of problem, such as strongly advising the parties to mediate their dispute, cutting off civil discovery, or relying on burdens of proof or other techniques of civil procedure to simplify the questions that it needs to answer. Courts can conceivably rely on expert witnesses or special masters as well. It is worth pointing out that it is conceivable that legal doctrine is held back here by judicial pride; it would be a rare judge that says to litigating parties, "Your contract is just too sophisticated and intricate for me to understand. I don't know enough, or am not smart enough, to resolve your dispute." Courts have held that legal doctrine is too difficult for reasonable *lawyers* to understand, *see* Lucas v. Hamm, 364 P.2d 685 (Cal. 1961) (holding that the rule against perpetuities is so difficult to understand that it is not malpractice for a lawyer to misunderstand it), but it is presumably harder for judges to say the same thing about themselves.

many US states, permits the development of an LLC that is governed *exclusively* by an operating agreement that defers major decisions to a running algorithm. This is achieved by producing, under existing statutes, an LLC that continues to exist even after its last member has dissociated. In other words, a perpetual LLC managed only by an algorithm is as simple as setting up a regular LLC whose operating agreement defers to an algorithm and then having all the members leave. Much as Douglas Adams described flying as "learning how to throw yourself at the ground and miss," a zero-member LLC is just a single-member LLC with one fewer member.

A zero-member LLC may seem radical, but it is just an incremental development in the flexible use of organizational statutes. Every similar incremental development in the past in the law of organizations – even the notion of single-member companies, which are now common-place – was one thought of as radical.[15] Zero-member LLCs may seem like a loophole, but they are a natural outgrowth of the flexibility that LLCs have intentionally been given by policymakers, and similar uses of algorithms have been specifically blessed by new state statutes.[16]

1.3 MODERN APPROACHES TO SOFTWARE "RIGHTS"

As a further demonstration that my approach is not as radical as it may first seem, in recent years there have been a variety of attempts around the world to give a form of personhood, or at least some types of binding legal recognition, to the partially or fully autonomous operation of software.

In a 2017 resolution, the European Parliament recommended that the European Commission consider adopting legal personhood for software systems directly and as an intentional legislative change. The evocatively worded resolution, which referred to Isaac Asimov's laws of robotics and began with "whereas" clauses like

---

[15] I mean this specifically, not just evocatively; see Chapter 4 (*infra* note 146) for examples of the horror with which commentators regarded the rise of single-person companies, which today are uncontroversial.

[16] *See infra* Section 1.3 and Chapter 4.

whereas from Mary Shelley's Frankenstein's Monster to the classical myth of Pygmalion, through the story of Prague's Golem to the
robot of Karel Čapek, who coined the word, people have fantasised
about the possibility of building intelligent machines, more often
than not androids with human features;

and

whereas now that humankind stands on the threshold of an era when
ever more sophisticated robots, bots, androids and other manifestations of artificial intelligence ("AI") seem to be poised to unleash a new
industrial revolution, which is likely to leave no stratum of society
untouched, it is vitally important for the legislature to consider its
legal and ethical implications and effects, without stifling innovation;

specifically proposed "creating a specific legal status for robots in the long
run, so that at least the most sophisticated autonomous robots could be
established as having the status of electronic persons responsible for
making good any damage they may cause, and possibly applying electronic personality to cases where robots make autonomous decisions or
otherwise interact with third parties independently."[17] This resolution
generated strong public opposition,[18] and the European Commission has
not adopted the European Parliament's recommendation to create a form
of legal personhood for software systems,[19] but its passage serves as
powerful evidence that consideration of the personhood for software has

---

[17] European Parliament Resolution of 16 February 2017 with Recommendations to the
Commission on Civil Law Rules on Robotics (2015/2103(INL)), available at www
.europarl.europa.eu/doceo/document/TA-8-2017-0051_EN.html [https://perma.cc
/Q6WM-LJMV].

[18] *E.g.*, *Open Letter to the European Commission: Artificial Intelligence and Robotics*, https://
g8fip1kplyr33r3krz5b97d1-wpengine.netdna-ssl.com/wp-content/uploads/2018/04/
RoboticsOpenLetter.pdf [https://perma.cc/J4UF-SRYV] (signed by many professors
throughout Europe). In my view the letter rested largely on formalistic ground. For
example, as the letter put it, "The legal status for a robot can't derive from the Legal
Entity model, since it implies the existence of human persons behind the legal person to
represent and direct it. And this is not the case for a robot." At least under US law, nothing
in the text, structure, scheme, function, or evident purpose of statutes requires the
"existence of human persons behind" the entities created. Indeed, from an American
perspective it is even unclear what "behind" means; even an autonomous entity may well
have humans associated with it or humans who "represent" it. The question of how
artificial systems of various types should interact with the legal system is properly one of
policy, not one of axiomatic derivation from fundamental concepts.

[19] *See* Thomas Burri, *The EU Is Right to Refuse Legal Personality for Artificial Intelligence*, www
.euractiv.com/section/digital/opinion/the-eu-is-right-to-refuse-legal-personality-for-

become a credible position in mainstream political discussion. It also demonstrates the importance of the subject, in view of the desires both to encourage innovation and to harmonize algorithms into a legal system that will regulate them properly – for example, by making systems liable for the harms they cause to others.

As a different sort of demonstration of explicit legal progress in favor of the ideas described in this book, in 2018 the state of Vermont passed a statute enabling "Blockchain-based Limited Liability Companies," thereby creating a new form of legal entity that "may provide for its governance, in whole or in part, through blockchain technology."[20] The phrase "in whole or in part" is an extraordinary statutory development; it explicitly recognizes that an LLC may be governed entirely, at least as a matter of internal governance (versus oversight by government), by software. The statute is odd in privileging one particular form of software system – blockchains – but that would not be a significant obstacle for organizers of a potential entity driven by other types of software systems: the concept of blockchains has become so flexible that any software-based decision-making scheme could be expressed as a blockchain even if it is not natively or internally structured as one.[21]

Though Vermont's statute is not framed in terms of granting "rights" or "personhood" to software, it is easy to see how permitting a company to be controlled by software "in whole or in part" permits software (so long as it is expressed in this case – again, somewhat arbitrarily – as a blockchain) to have immediate legal effect. As

---

artificial-intelligence/ [https://perma.cc/4XTU-7XCZ], May 31, 2018, reporting the developments and arguing that the European Commission was correct not to follow the European Parliament's resolution, but not for the usual reasons that generated public opposition to the European Parliament's resolution. Instead, Professor Burri argued that under EU law, it is the member states and not the institutions of the EU that properly define the nature of legal personhood. He also argued that the techniques described in the research that led up to this book make the resolution unnecessary; that is, if functional legal personhood can already be achieved using the techniques in Chapter 3, there is no need for legislative change.

[20] 11 VT. STAT. ANN. §§ 4173 et seq.

[21] Vermont's statute explicitly permits "any reasonable algorithmic means for accomplishing the consensus process for validating records." 11 VT. STAT. ANN. § 4175. To elaborate the technical observation in the text, it would not be difficult to produce a blockchain "shell" or "wrapper" around any other algorithm – for example, by having an existing algorithm be executed, confirmed, or otherwise recognized by a distributed system that produced a chain of blocks – and that should be sufficient for Vermont's statute.

Chapter 2 will explain in more detail, giving software a direct legal effect is the same thing as giving it the limited "rights" of private-law personhood. For example, just as by signing a written agreement a human can cause a legally binding contract to be formed, under Vermont's statute the operation of a blockchain can cause a company to take binding legal action.

Both the European Parliament's endeavor and the Vermont statutes appear to be motivated in large part by the recognition of the promise of technology. But neither the European Parliament nor the Vermont legislature had a utopian view, and neither ignored the potential costs of technological development. Under conventional legal understanding, something that is not a legal person cannot be sued or be held liable by courts, and the European Parliament's resolution justifies its innovation toward electronic personhood partly in terms of the opportunity to impose liability for harms that algorithms may cause. For its part, Vermont's statute – which presumably was designed to attract blockchain-based businesses to organize in Vermont – is concerned about sensible regulation of software-based business too. It provides that the statute "does not exempt a [blockchain-based LLC] from any other judicial, statutory, or regulatory provision of Vermont law or federal law,"[22] so that an entity created under the statute will specifically be subject to the general laws that govern conventional LLCs in Vermont.

The lesson is that like all technologies, artificial intelligence and other forms of legally significant software will have benefits and costs, but it is better to recognize them (and incorporate them sensibly into the legal system) than either to ignore their costs or to focus so intently on their costs so as to stifle technological progress.

1.4 A COMMENT ON "RIGHTS" AND "PERSONHOOD"

The conventional language of private-law "rights" and "personhood" may be distracting when applied to artificial intelligence. Indeed, in my experience, the terminology of rights and personhood alone can be enough to raise strong opposition to the idea that artificial systems

---

[22] 11 Vt. Stat. Ann. § 4176.

should be able to interact with the legal system. Perhaps it would be better for this reason to write of "titleholders of legal property" and "automated contractors" rather than of rights and legal personhood, but I have opted for the conventional language because it is clearer, more general, and tends to obfuscate less.

It is worth keeping in mind, however, that these are legal terms of art. As I indicated earlier, this book's concern is not with the dimension of legal personhood that has recently become politicized in the United States; that is, my focus is not on questions like whether corporations have rights to donate to political campaigns or whether they can avail themselves of the protections that the First Amendment affords to religion.[23] As I describe in more detail in Chapter 5, nobody believes that "legal personhood" must confer *all* rights that natural people have (like the right to vote or marry).

In other words, I use the terminology of rights and personhood in this book simply to refer to the ability of algorithms and other systems to interact with the legal system at all – to be liable for breach of contract, to "own" legal property in order to be able to use it commercially or transfer it, and so on. That type of basic interaction should raise less concern about the "indignity" associated with granting rights to software, a topic that Chapter 5 discusses at some length.

There may come a time when we want to grant legal and other sorts of rights to artificial beings because we recognize their own goals and intrinsic worth – and one long-term advantage of my conceptual approach is that it may be useful on that day too – but for now the purpose of granting legal capabilities to software is to achieve what are, fundamentally, conventional human goals: convenience, efficiency, transactional and organizational flexibility, innovation, and so on.

1.5 LAYOUT OF THE BOOK

The rest of the book proceeds as follows.

Chapter 2 lays out in more detail the ways that legal instruments and agreements can use the notion of conditions to give legal effects to

---

[23] *See supra* note 3 and accompanying text.

algorithms, both in simple contractual structures and in more complex arrangements. It describes what I have sometimes called the "algorithm-agreement equivalence principle," which is the notion that algorithms and agreements are really, in many respects, the same thing, or at least that they operate at similar levels of abstraction, may serve similar roles, and can often substitute for one another.

Chapter 3 introduces the core legal mechanism that enables autonomous organizations under current US law: the combination of the transactional techniques of Chapter 2 with the creation of a perpetual LLC, or at least an LLC of arbitrary or indefinite duration, that has no members and thus is controlled only by agreement – and thus by algorithm.

Chapter 4 explains, in terms of legal doctrine, why the techniques of Chapter 3 will succeed as a matter of law. A reaction to the ideas of Chapter 3 that is common among lawyers is something to the effect of: "This is crazy. It's just a loophole. Judges will find a way to strike it down." (Some reactions have been even stronger; Professor Lynn LoPucki of UCLA has suggested in a law-review article that the "survival of the human race may depend" on finding a way to strike down Chapter 3's techniques.)[24] Clearly, I am more optimistic about these techniques. The goal of Chapter 4 is to explain why judges are unlikely to strike down autonomous organizations and probably, for practical reasons, couldn't even if they wanted to. It also argues that statutory reform against autonomous organizations would be exceedingly difficult to achieve, even if there were a public will to do so – and all indications are that the statutory tendency is in fact in the other direction, *toward* giving software the power to influence the operation of organizations. And it observes that even if zero-member LLCs are problematic for any reason, people who wish to set up autonomous organizations can do so in a variety of other ways and would just need one jurisdiction to approve their technique in order for their organizations to function. As a result, there is virtually no way to prevent autonomous organizations, short of a massive, coordinated, and unlikely law-reform effort by many different legal jurisdictions.

---

[24] Lynn M. LoPucki, *Algorithmic Entities*, 95 WASH. U. L. REV. 887 (2018) (responding to my earlier articles on this subject).

Chapter 5 moves from legal doctrine to legal policy: it defends my approach to autonomous organizations in terms of its costs and benefits and the costs and benefits of alternative regulatory approaches (including one that simply ignores the possibility of a greater role for software in operating legal organizations).

Finally, Chapter 6 discusses the outer edges of my approach – the consequences, including negative consequences, of my ideas. That is, it discusses implications for other areas of law of the possibility of autonomous organizations, such as an appropriately reduced role for the concept of "intent" in civil law and the importance of a robust set of doctrines for managing the drift between original, hard-to-change agreements and facts that later develop, potentially long after the agreements were made.

2 THE LEGAL ROLE OF ALGORITHMS

In trying to figure out how the law can accommodate algorithms, there has been a persistent drive to compare algorithms to legal agents – that is, to people who execute the wishes of a principal who sets transactions in motion.[25] The informal analogy is clear enough; a business might replace employees with automated software or hardware, and the analogy between a "digital assistant" from Apple or Amazon and a human "personal assistant" seems intuitive, though strained in the details.

The law has a special recognition and a significant doctrine of legal agency, however – covering the opportunity for one person to act for another person's interests – and that body of law is a poor fit to the function of algorithms that operate "on behalf of" businesses. Under

---

[25] *See, e.g.*, Emad Abdel Rahim Dahiyat, *Artificial Intelligence and Law: Do We Need a Thoughtful Reconsideration?*, 8 COLO. TECH. L.J. 351, 376–81 (2020) (evaluating several earlier arguments); Lauren Henry Scholz, *Algorithmic Contracts*, 20 STAN. TECH. L. REV. 128 (2017) (providing "an agency approach to the formation of algorithmic contracts"); SAMIR CHOPRA & LAURENCE F. WHITE, A LEGAL THEORY FOR AUTONOMOUS ARTIFICIAL AGENTS (2011); Samir Chopra & Laurence White, *Artificial Agents and the Contracting Problem: A Solution Via an Agency Analysis*, 2009 U. ILL. J.L. TECH. & POL'Y 363, 403 ("We conclude that the application of the common-law doctrine of agency to the contracting problem involving artificial agents is cogent, viable and doctrinally satisfying."); Ian Kerr, *Spirits in the Material World: Intelligent Agents As Intermediaries in Electronic Commerce*, 22 DALHOUSIE L.J. 189, 241 (1999) ("Having established a credible basis for the electronic agent metaphor, it is important to determine which of the various principles of agency law are relevant to electronic commerce."); Suzanne Smed, *Intelligent Software Agents and Agency Law*, 14 SANTA CLARA HIGH TECH. L.J. 503, 504 (1998) ("[I]ntelligent software agents should be regulated under agency law."); John P. Fischer, *Computers as Agents: A Proposed Approach to Revised U.C.C. Article 2*, 72 IND. L.J. 545 (1997).

current law, algorithms are not agents, and trying to treat them as agents serves little purpose and raises a variety of intractable problems.

Instead, the law already has a clean way to accommodate algorithms: legal instruments (such as LLC operating agreements) and legal contracts can recognize algorithms directly, by recognizing their state or output as conditions for legal obligations to take effect. For example, just as a home-purchase contract might say, "The buyer's obligation to purchase this home is conditioned on an inspection that is satisfactory to the buyer," a similar contract might provide, "The buyer's obligation to purchase this home is conditioned on the output of a particular algorithm that indicates that the home has passed the algorithm's inspection."[26] Recognizing this possible interaction between law and algorithm lays the groundwork for a considerably more flexible, adaptive way to harmonize algorithms into the existing legal system than the law of agency. The algorithm is simply the basis for or expression of a contractual condition; it is unnecessary and unhelpful to ask whose "agent" the algorithm is.

Similarly, suppose a company uses a sophisticated software system to determine what contracts to enter into with counterparties in a large, online contractual marketplace. Some of the company's competitors might use individual people to perform similar analysis, but our sample company has decided it will benefit from automating its contracting process. It is tempting to say – and many commentators have suggested[27] – that just like the humans for which it logically substitutes, the software system is an "agent" making contracts on behalf of the company, which the law calls a "principal." My argument is that this is in fact not a useful way to analyze the relationship between the company and its software system: it clashes with existing law, creates a number of tricky legal ambiguities, and serves little function overall. Instead, it is more helpful, and more in line with existing law, to treat the company's software system as being given legal effect by the company's agreements or other legal instruments.

---

[26] Indeed, the seller is likely to prefer the latter because it replaces a question of the buyer's satisfaction (which often has a complex objective dimension because it depends on the buyer's *reasonable* satisfaction) with an entirely objective one that is easy to verify.

[27] *See supra* note 25.

"Agreements" in the sense I am describing them amount to quite a general class of legal activities. They include the simple two-party contracts I have been using as an example, but they also include operating agreements of companies or trust agreements. Indeed, the concept I have been describing applies to more or less any legal instrument, at least in theory. So, for example, a statute, regulation, or legal judgment might, at least in principle, recognize the verifiable states of software as conditions for the rights or duties they create to come into effect. Under US law, statutes that attempt this may face arcane constitution restrictions on the "delegation" of legislative powers,[28] but it is unremarkable in the general case for a legal agreement or instrument to specify or recognize a series of obligations or conditions computed by a complex formula with inputs whose future values are not known when the agreement or instrument is produced.

The principles I have just described lead, perhaps almost mundanely, to an idea that has seemed revolutionary to many, which is that the operating agreements of legal entities (such as an LLC) can be used to give effect to the verifiable states of algorithms. As Chapter 3 describes, the result is that algorithms can effectively act in any way that a legal entity can act. But for now, the consequences needn't be so grandiose. For example, a relatively conventional business organization could operate under a charter that restricts its activities (or the activities of a division of the organization) based on the verifiable state of algorithms – anything from a simple program that produces a descriptive statistic based on mundane data to the output of a complex neural net. Similarly, part of a conventional legal entity's operation may be automated; a company might sell food to distributors in manually negotiated contracts but also sell it automatically, via vending machines or a website, to individual consumers, and not all such sales need human thought or action for them to be legally binding.

---

[28] *E.g.*, INS v. Chadha, 462 US 919, 944 (1983) (invalidating a statute as unconstitutional, despite "[c]onvenience and efficiency," because of excessive "delegation" of powers from Congress to the Executive Branch). The Supreme Court's doctrine that powers are nondelegable has always struck me as formalistic and unjustified; there is nothing undemocratic about a legislature passing a statute that implements its goals by means of broad conditions, some of which are not under the legislature's ongoing control. *See* Eric A. Posner & Adrian Vermeule, *Interring the Nondelegation Doctrine*, 69 U. CHI. L. REV. 1721 (2002).

This chapter explains this concept in more detail, because it is a foundational concept for the demonstration, in Chapter 3, that a software system can "inhabit" a legal person like an LLC.

2.1 ALGORITHM AS AGREEMENT

This chapter's thesis is simple: as a general matter, agreements are a functional and conceptually straightforward way for the law to recognize algorithms. In particular, using agreements to welcome algorithms into the law is better than trying to use the law of agency to do so.[29] Casual speech and conceptualism have led to the commonplace notion of "electronic agents," but the law of agreements is a more functional entry point for algorithms to interact with the law than the concept of vicarious action. Algorithms need not involve any vicarious action, and most of the law of agency translates very poorly to algorithms that lack intent, reasonable understanding, and legal personality in their own right; instead, algorithms cause activity that may have contractual or other agreement-based legal significance.[30] Recognizing the power (and perhaps the necessity) of addressing algorithms flexibly by means of the law governing agreements and other legal instruments can free us from formalistic attempts to shoehorn algorithms into a limited set of existing legal categories.

The principle that algorithms are coordinate in scope and function to legal agreements may initially seem surprising, but even as a casual, intuitive matter, it is not difficult to see the correspondence. For example, I commonly advise law students who have computer-science backgrounds that writing contracts or operating agreements involves very similar skills to writing software: both require accounting for different

---

[29] For the last few decades, commentators have offered a wide variety of conceptual models, including human agents (*see supra* note 25), as candidates for the law's analogical treatment of algorithms, artificial intelligence, autonomous systems, and similar innovations. *See, e.g.*, Matthew U. Scherer, *Of Wild Beasts and Digital Analogues: The Legal Status of Autonomous Systems*, 19 NEV. L.J. 259 (2018) (considering different conceptual models by means of which the way may recognize algorithms, including children, animals, and legal agents); Sam N. Lehman-Wilzig, *Frankenstein Unbound: Towards a Legal Definition of Artificial Intelligence*, 13 FUTURES 442 (1981) (surveying the same conceptual models and others).

[30] To be sure, the autonomous organizations described in the next chapter can indeed serve as legal agents, just as they can execute the other capabilities of legal persons.

possible future states, addressing them with logic and structure, and then releasing an attempt at a solution into an uncertain world. As the computer scientist Alan Perlis once put it, "Programmers are not to be measured by their ingenuity and their logic but by the completeness of their case analysis,"[31] and that (debatable) proposition applies with similar (debatable) force, and for the same reasons, to transactional lawyers. Both algorithms and legal agreements can have "bugs" that result from logical errors or errors in anticipating events; writing both clearly and manageably is a rare, creative skill too often neglected; in practical settings, producing both relies on significant reuse of prior work, based on a wealth of (often public) professional experience recorded in written form; the generation of both can be automated (a point not sufficiently recognized either for agreements or for software);[32] and so on.

My point is not just intuitive or loosely analogical, however; it is analytical: any algorithm with verifiable states can be expressed, or recognized, by a legal agreement. (For my purposes, "verifiable state" has the same meaning as it does in economic contract theory: state that can be proven to the court that would enforce the agreement.[33] If the state of an algorithm is not verifiable to third parties like courts, it is unclear how or whether the law can recognize it.) This capability of agreements follows from the legal proposition that agreements can recognize, and vary legal rights based on, verifiable conditions – that is, states of the world. States of the world include states of algorithmic processes. Accordingly, legal agreements can give effect to the verifiable states of algorithms.

Of course, I don't mean to imply that any legal agreement must be enforceable; a court might, for example, strike down an agreement on grounds of public policy regardless of whether it happens to contain

---

[31] Alan Perlis, *Epigrams in Programming*, ACM SIGPLAN NOTICES, Sept. 1982, at 7.

[32] For software, a helpful demonstration of this principle appears in BRIAN KERNIGHAN & ROB PIKE, THE PRACTICE OF PROGRAMMING 237–45 (1999). For legal documents, I elaborate the notion later in this section.

[33] For an introduction to and modern critique of the distinction between "verifiable" and "observable" information under economic contract theory, see Hans Lind & Johan Nystrom, *The Explanation of Incomplete Contracts in Mainstream Contract Theory: A Critique of the Distinction between "Observable" and "Verifiable,"* 7 J. EVOLUT. INST. ECON. REV. 279 (2011). In short, *verifiable* information can be proved to courts; *observable* information may be witnessed by others but not necessarily provable to courts.

conditions based on algorithmic processing. My point is simply that legal agreements can depend on the execution of algorithms. Moreover, sufficiently precise agreements may be expressed as algorithms; there is no conceptual difference, other than perhaps the level of precision, between an agreement that sets up procedures to manage contractual performance and an algorithm.[34]

A few demonstrations of this notion may be helpful. To begin with, as background, in some sense highly automated contracts have existed for decades, treated as almost mundane by the legal system and by all the parties involved. For example, a labor union's contract with an employer may schedule complex salary increases according to an algorithmic formula, which is implemented with little human oversight; nobody would seriously dispute that employees are owed the salary increases that the algorithm has produced. At least one of my colleagues – perhaps most of them – have no idea what they are paid and never look personally at the details of their paychecks; at many employers, at least some salary increases happen automatically, without any necessary human attention to the individual raises being applied to employees; as a result, there are almost certainly specific salary increases that no human is aware of but which are nonetheless unproblematically binding as legal matter. Stock trades are executed automatically all the time between computer programs, and individual traders are happy to say "fill my order at the market price" knowing that that price is the result, at least in part, of algorithmic processes. Consumers routinely buy goods and services – for example, airline tickets, or merchandise through an online retailer – using prices set by complex algorithms. And so on.

Software can play a more general role in contracts, though; it can cause them to come into existence in the first place, rather than simply implementing the technical details (like pay increases) of a contract.

---

[34] Not every agreement can be implemented literally by an algorithm, but that is mainly because agreements may not be precise enough to qualify as algorithms. Some agreements may be more analogous to a functional specification for an algorithm than an algorithm, or to a general discussion of an algorithm among nonprogrammers. When I claim that agreements are in some sense interchangeable or "isomorphic" with algorithms, I mean only (1) that any that any agreement can be expressed by an algorithm as specifically as the precision of the agreement allows and (2) more loosely, that agreements and algorithms operate at a similar level of generality.

Consider an algorithm that produces, from many inputs, a single scalar output[35] that is meant to embody a price that the legal entity that runs the algorithm is willing to pay for a commodity. Legal agreements, such as simple contracts, can depend on this output in a variety of ways. One simple way is for the legal entity to print (or record in electronic form) a contractual offer – a precursor to a legal agreement – using a templating (or "mail merge") system that substitutes the algorithm's price in place of a generic marker when generating the offer document.[36] Such a document would be indistinguishable, on its face, from one that did not depend on the output of an algorithm, much as a web browser has no way in the general case to know whether a page it has received is a copy of static text or the product of a dynamic system.[37]

Of course, the offer might instead refer explicitly to the current state of an algorithm rather than include a prior, static output: it might say "Our offer is to buy 100 units of this good at the price our algorithm has currently posted at the time you accept this offer." Such an offer, and the legal contract that may result from it, should be entirely unremarkable to lawyers and businesspeople; it is hard to see a serious objection to the role that an algorithm has played in the generation of such contracts, and indeed references to changing prices and other terms outside a particular contractual document (or a particular set of prior communications between the parties) were commonplace, and taught in first-year Contracts classes, long before anyone spoke of algorithmic contracts.[38]

---

[35] Computer scientists and programmers borrow the term "scalar" from linear algebra to refer to a single data item, commonly a real number.

[36] In pseudocode for a templating language, this might look like "We propose to buy 100 units from you at $price."

[37] I have explained this concept in detail to novice computer programmers, for pedagogical purposes, in SHAWN BAYERN, JSTL IN ACTION 4–14 (2003).

[38] See Nanakuli Paving & Rock Co. v. Shell Oil Co., 664 F.2d 772, 778 (interpreting a written contract that referred to "Shell's Posted Price at time of delivery"). To be clear, and contrary perhaps to some people's intuitive notion of the law, modern contract law does not require that parties fix a numeric price at the time of contract formation, and indeed they may not have any specific idea of the price and may explicitly wish to defer its determination. See, e.g., U.C.C. § 2–305(1) ("The parties if they so intend can conclude a contract for sale even though the price is not settled."); RESTATEMENT (SECOND) OF CONTRACTS § 33 cmt. e (1981) (referring to the U.C.C., which governs sales of goods, and noting that "[s]imilar principles apply to contracts for the rendition of service").

It is easy to generalize this concept to apply to multiple outputs rather than a single output.[39] It also turns out to be easy to generalize it to stages in the contracting process other than the insertion of conditions into an offer. For example, an algorithm might choose when to generate an offer document (or whether and when to legally accept one sent to it) and might communicate with its legal entity's contractual counterparties itself.

One question that may arise in the day-to-day use of agreements that recognize the operation of software is how to authenticate that software – that is, how to identify and confirm the specific software that the agreement recognizes and how to resolve disputes if there are multiple candidates for that software or its operational state. As a general matter, agreements will simply need to be as precise as practical concerns dictate. Cryptography and high-grade computer security can be used (i.e., deployed in practice and specified carefully in legal agreements) if necessary, but they are not always necessary. The problem of authenticating the state of algorithms may track the debate a few decades ago about how conventional agreements would need to be "signed" as they moved from paper to the internet; many people assumed that public-key infrastructures or other heavyweight technological solutions would be needed, but in practice scanning physical signatures, clicking buttons in DocuSign, or simply typing names at the end of emails turned out to be secure and reliable enough in most situations. Indeed, the law today doesn't care what mode of signature is used; its goal is to be flexible because it is difficult to predict in advance the particular circumstances of a wide range of contracting parties.[40] As the Uniform Electronic Transactions Act (UETA) put it

---

[39] Again, in pseudocode for a general templating language, this might look like "Dear $customer: We propose that you buy $quantity units at $price on $date. Please see our warranty terms below: $terms[$customer]. Sincerely, Offeror."

[40] Signatures do not matter as much in contract law as laypeople often assume they do. Their main function is to satisfy the Statute of Frauds, a rule of law that restricts the enforcement of some (but only some) types of contracts unless there is a "writing" (not necessarily the "contract" and not necessarily even a written document) signed by the person who opposes enforcement of the contract. As further background, in US contract law a "contract" does not refer to a written agreement but, more generally, to any enforceable promise. See RESTATEMENT (SECOND) OF CONTRACTS § 1 ("A contract is a promise or a set of promises for the breach of which the law gives a remedy, or the performance of which the law in some way recognizes as a duty.").

in 1999, "No specific technology need be used in order to create a valid signature. One's voice on an answering machine may suffice if the requisite intention is present. Similarly, including one's name as part of an electronic mail communication also may suffice, as may the firm name on a facsimile."[41] (The only thing that has aged badly about that passage is its reference to fax machines.)

Authenticating the identity and state of algorithms can be similarly flexible. Obviously, particular applications that demand more security and more careful authentication can use it, but the experience of contract law and practice is that even significant business deals can be concluded using relatively informal means. Most people are basically honest, and the civil and criminal penalties against fraud are enough to deter most abuses.

In short, anyone who seeks to write a condition that depends on an algorithm into a legal instrument can identify the algorithm with varying degrees of formality. As a demonstration of this flexibility, and to make the possibilities more concrete, all the following candidates for contractual language, increasing roughly in order of formality, should pose no problems for the law: (1) "as posted on our website"; (2) "as displayed on the computer screen located on the nineteenth floor of 417 Grand Street"; (3) "as running on the server at `essentially.net`"; (4) "the last entry before 5:00 p.m. each Friday, GMT −0500, recorded in `/usr/local/etc/algorithm.out` in the Linode[42] instance named `essentially_net` within the account registered to the undersigned party"; (5) "any signed messages addressed to the RSA public key included as Appendix A to this agreement and received as described in the network protocol specified in Appendix B to this agreement." As with any legal instrument, the goal is just to specify every contractual condition with enough specificity to address any plausibly important concerns; the need for contractual precision and technological authentication will depend on the economic or other stakes of the contractual condition at issue and on the perceived likelihood of its abuse.

---

[41] UNIF. ELECTRONIC TRANSACTIONS ACT § 2 cmt. (1999). UETA is adopted in the vast majority of US states. *Cf. also* Jane K. Winn, *The Emperor's New Clothes: The Shocking Truth About Digital Signatures and Internet Commerce*, 37 IDAHO L. REV. 353 (2001).

[42] Linode is a provider of cloud-computing services.

2.2 ALGORITHMS AS A COMPREHENSIVE BASIS FOR CONTRACT FORMATION

It is easy to see how specific contractual provisions might require approval from or otherwise depend on a software system. Again, in the simplest case, an agreement could read, "You have this particular duty only in the event that our software system outputs the following text when presented with the particular inquiry copied as Appendix A to this instrument."

But it is also not difficult to generalize from this capability of private law to a significantly more general one: the ability for software to direct, generally, arbitrary contractual processes. For example, suppose a corporation wishes to replace a human salesperson, who acts formally as an agent in causing the corporation to enter contracts, with an artificially intelligent computer program. Under the generally received understanding of private law, the software cannot literally step into the human's role and serve as an agent. For example, as the official comment to the *Restatement (Third) of Agency* puts it, a

> computer program is not capable of acting as a principal or an agent as defined by the common law. At present, computer programs are instrumentalities of the persons who use them. If a program malfunctions even in ways unanticipated by its designer or user, the legal consequences for the person who uses it are no different than the consequences stemming from the malfunction of any other type of instrumentality.[43]

However, the computer program need not have the formal legal powers of an agent in order to have the effects that the corporation wants it to have. Suppose the corporation in our example enters into a structural agreement with potential buyers, saying, in effect, "Under this agreement, orders become effective when our computerized agent submits a document to you and you approve its terms." I draw the term "structural agreement" from the work of Mel Eisenberg, a leading scholar of contract law, who describes the notion (as applied to general business dealings, not those involving artificial intelligences) as follows:

---

[43] *See* RESTATEMENT (THIRD) OF AGENCY § 1.04 cmt. e (2006).

In [one] kind of promissory structure, one party makes a promise that increases the probability of exchange, but that promise does not require either a promise or an act in exchange. I call such promissory structures structural agreements.

Under the bargain principle, bargains between capable and informed actors are enforced according to their terms. This principle rests in large part on the premises that bargains produce gains through trade, that capable and informed actors are normally the best judges of their own utilities, and that those utilities are revealed in the terms of the parties' bargain.

Although the bargain principle is most conventionally applied to classical bargains, it applies to structural agreements as well. Structural agreements, like classical bargains, involve promises designed to promote economic exchange. The terms of structural agreements, like the terms of classical bargains, are normally bargained out. And as in the case of classical bargains, the promisor in a structural agreement makes his promise because it will serve his economic interest. Reasons comparable to those for enforcing classical bargains are therefore applicable to structural agreements: structural agreements are entered into to produce gains through trade; a capable and informed actor is normally the best judge of his own utility; and that utility is revealed in the terms of his agreement.[44]

Consider, then, a structural agreement that specifically enables software, including artificially intelligent software. The (human) parties or agents have negotiated such an agreement, and the agreement provides that one party's software will supply documents to be approved by the other party (or its software) and that when this happens the parties will have a binding agreement. If such an agreement is enforceable, then once it is in place all further steps of the negotiation, practically speaking, could occur between computer programs, and the background contractual framework provides a mechanism to produce legally enforceable contracts.

In recent work, my colleague Lauren Scholz has nicely suggested a potential complication for this approach: perhaps the common-law

---

[44] Melvin Aron Eisenberg, *Probability and Chance in Contract Law*, 45 UCLA L. Rev. 1005, 1009–10 (1998). Professor Eisenberg describes in detail why the classical, formal doctrine of consideration should not invalidate such agreements under modern law.

courts would reject such contracts for reasons associated with classical doctrines of contract law.[45] Professor Scholz's main challenge to a scheme like the one I have outlined here is that it may be too indefinite to be enforced. There are other potential pitfalls; for example, perhaps courts would have trouble with the legal-doctrinal mechanisms of offer and acceptance under the scheme I've outlined, or perhaps they would treat the structural agreement as illusory and therefore lacking consideration.[46] Similarly, perhaps it would simply be an unenforceable "agreement to agree."[47]

For three reasons, however, I don't see significant barriers to at least American courts' enforcement of these contracts. First, classical contract law is on the decline, and the formalist doctrines have eroded as significant barriers to the enforcement of agreements made in a commercial setting.[48] Consideration doctrine, for example, is best seen under modern law as a way to distinguish gifts from commercial promises, and courts and the leading treatises have shifted away from

---

[45] Scholz, *supra* note 25.

[46] *Cf.* Eisenberg, *supra* note 44, at 1011–21 (sharply critiquing the use of consideration doctrine for this purpose in modern contexts).

[47] Such inchoate agreements were not enforceable under classical law, although modern law, with an emphasis on commercial function rather than formal principles of contract formation, has had considerably less trouble enforcing them. *See generally* RESTATEMENT (SECOND) OF CONTRACTS § 33(2) ("The terms of a contract are reasonably certain if they provide a basis for determining the existence of a breach and for giving an appropriate remedy."); U.C.C. § 2-204(3) ("Even though one or more terms are left open a contract for sale does not fail for indefiniteness if the parties have intended to make a contract and there is a reasonably certain basis for giving an appropriate remedy."); *id.* § 2-305 cmt. 1 ("This Article rejects in these instances the formula that 'an agreement to agree is unenforceable' if the case falls within subsection (1) of this section, and rejects also defeating such agreements on the ground of 'indefiniteness'.").

[48] With reference to consideration doctrines based on "mutuality" and the "illusory-promise rule" – that is, the main obstacle to the enforceability of structural agreements – see, for example, Helle v. Landmark, Inc., 472 N.E.2d 765, 776 (Ohio 1984) ("As a contract defense, the mutuality doctrine has become a faltering rampart to which a litigant retreats at his own peril. Under contemporary analysis of unilateral contracts, the 'mutuality' doctrine crumbles of its own weight.") (citing several leading modern treatises); Tex. Gas Utils. Co. v. Barrett, 460 S.W.2d 409, 412 (Tex. 1970) ("It is presumed that when parties make an agreement they intend it to be effectual, not nugatory. A contract will be construed in favor of mutuality. The modern decisional tendency is against lending the aid of courts to defeat contracts on technical grounds of want of mutuality.") (citations omitted). *See also* Eisenberg, *supra* note 44, at 1011–21; Shawn Bayern, *Offer and Acceptance in Modern Contract Law: A Needless Concept*, 103 CAL. L. REV. 67, 90–93 (2015).

the strictures of the classical doctrine.[49] According to *Corbin on Contracts*, "Consideration is designed primarily to protect promisors from their own donative promises"[50] rather than to serve to invalidate commercial bargains. And in general, modern law treats contracts as being definite enough to enforce even when they leave significant terms and conditions open to future development; the modern rule is only that the contract needs to be certain enough for a court (1) to distinguish performance from breach and (2) to fashion an appropriate remedy.[51]

Second, there needs to be just one state that enforces the form of agreement I have described for it to become commercially significant, given parties' ability to choose the law that governs their contractual arrangements. States do split on matters of contract doctrine, with some being relatively more formalistic and some more functionalistic, but if one state upholds structural agreements that give software the power to take contractual actions by means of contractual conditions, then parties can effectively deploy such agreements. Indeed, states might seek to become friendly to this type of agreement in order to attract business, just as Vermont and Wyoming have adopted laws friendly to blockchain technologies.[52]

Third, very broadly, the common law over time has yielded to commercial pressures. If two parties enter into what is otherwise a fair agreement, without fraud, duress, unconscionability, or anything similar, it is easy to see many modern courts enforcing the agreement even if it is unconventional.[53]

---

[49] *See* Melvin Aron Eisenberg, *The World of Contract and the World of Gift*, 85 CAL. L. REV. 821 (1997).

[50] 2 ARTHUR CORBIN ET AL, CORBIN ON CONTRACTS § 5.17 (rev. ed. 1995) (cited approvingly in 1484-Eight, Ltd. & Millis Management Corp. v. Joppich, 152 S.W.3d 101 (Tex. 2004)).

[51] *See supra* note 38; RESTATEMENT (SECOND) OF CONTRACTS § 33(2) ("The terms of a contract are reasonably certain if they provide a basis for determining the existence of a breach and for giving an appropriate remedy.").

[52] Jason Tashea, *Wyoming and Vermont Hope to Attract Tech Entrepreneurs by Passing Laws Favorable to Blockchain*, ABA J., Mar. 1, 2019, www.abajournal.com/magazine/article/ blockchain-wyoming-vermont-regulations-laws [https://perma.cc/LD4F-XL5W]; *see also supra note* 12.

[53] *Cf.* Shawn Bayern, Thomas Burri et al., *Company Law and Autonomous Systems: A Blueprint for Lawyers, Entrepreneurs, and Regulators*, 9 HASTINGS SCI. & TECH. L.J. 135, 152 (2017) ("U.K. courts have taken a pragmatic approach to the development and use of corporate personalities in the past. Taken forward, this flexibility could readily accommodate technological advances in artificial intelligence.").

Other, relatively nonstandard doctrines of some states' contract law may appear to impose barriers to software-driven contracts in a way that might pose problems for autonomous organizations, but they are probably not significant. Consider, for instance, a policy by some courts to disfavor contracts that are "perpetual." Several state courts have explicitly stated this policy in their contract jurisprudence,[54] but those same states have statutes that clearly permit some organizations to last forever.[55] In any event, an interpretive policy disfavoring perpetual contracts is not difficult for most parties to work around; ordinarily they can do so simply by making the contract's intended perpetual nature explicit.[56]

So far, I have described a mechanism by which the *existing* legal agents of companies can effectively authorize a computer program to enter into *future* contractual arrangements even though the computer program lacks any formal legal status as an agent. But there is a further step if software is to act comprehensively under the common law of contracts: can software create entirely new contracts with entirely new contracting partners – that is, without the preexistence of the sort of structural agreement I have described, and thus without the involvement of any human to initialize the agreement?

The Uniform Electronic Transaction Act (UETA), adopted by the vast majority of US states, answers that question affirmatively: "A contract may be formed by the interaction of electronic agents of the parties, even if no individual was aware of or reviewed the electronic agents' actions or the resulting terms and agreements."[57] Moreover,

---

[54] *E.g.*, MS Real Estate Holdings, LLC v. Donald P. Fox Family Tr., 864 N.W.2d 83, 93 (Wis. 2015) (referring to "Wisconsin's policy disfavoring perpetual contracts"); Wyeth Pharm., Inc. v. Borough of W. Chester, 126 A.3d 1055, 1064 (Pa. Commw. Ct. 2015) ("Pennsylvania law disfavors perpetual contracts and, thus, requires a perpetual term to be expressed unequivocally."); *see also* 17A AM. JUR. 2D CONTRACTS § 457 (collecting sources on this topic).

[55] *E.g.*, WIS. STAT. § 180.0301(c) ("Unless its articles of incorporation provide otherwise, a corporation has perpetual duration ... ."); 15 PENN. CONS. STAT. § 8818 (2016) ("A limited liability company has perpetual duration.").

[56] *E.g.*, *Wyeth Pharm*, 126 A.3d at 1064 ("In general, a contract for an indefinite period will be construed to be for a reasonable time or terminable at will *unless the intention of the parties can be ascertained.*") (emphasis added; internal quotations and citations omitted).

[57] UETA § 14(1); *see also id.* § 2 (defining "automated transaction" as "a transaction conducted or performed, in whole or in part, by electronic means or electronic records, in which the acts or records of one or both parties are not reviewed by an individual in the

contracts can be formed by the interactions between software and individuals,[58] even where the parties haven't previously interacted before. Of course, this should be no surprise, or else everyone who thinks they're buying food from a vending machine is in fact making an unaccepted contractual offer and then stealing the food.

Even apart from statutory law, general contract principles work in favor of forming and enforcing automated contracts. This is important because UETA doesn't itself replace contract law, and normal principles of contract law apply to the automated contracts created under UETA.[59] So if underlying contract law were unfriendly to or confused by these agreements, that might pose practical problems for them.

Still, even without UETA, there are several reasons to think that, for example, two companies could contractually commit to enter a joint venture with each other only because software programs used by both of them communicated with each other and made an agreement to do so, without any involvement from humans on either side. That is, there are several creative ways for software to have a comprehensive role in contract formation under conventional law. These techniques may seem almost mundane, but in some ways that is the point: the law already supports them, and courts would have a hard time interfering with them even if they were motivated to do so despite general trends and UETA's policy.

For example, standardized contractual terms on forms provide one possibility, at least to the extent they are enforceable. Suppose the company in our example that wishes to use a computer system to make contracts posts form terms on its website, saying, effectively, "If you take the following actions on our website, you agree to the following structural contract under which, if you submit a document to our software and the software approves it, we have a binding

ordinary course in forming a contract, performing under an existing contract, or fulfilling an obligation required by the transaction").

[58] *Id.* § 14(2) ("A contract may be formed by the interaction of an electronic agent and an individual, acting on the individual's own behalf or for another person, including by an interaction in which the individual performs actions that the individual is free to refuse to perform and which the individual knows or has reason to know will cause the electronic agent to complete the transaction or performance."); *see also id.* § 10(2) (laying out a protection for humans when they form, or purportedly form, contracts with software).

[59] *Id.* § 14(3).

agreement." Then, suppose another program accesses the website (and, perhaps, does something to indicate assent – essentially an automated protocol's equivalent of an "I Agree" button). Such a mechanism could be used to create a new structural agreement between two previously unconnected parties, and more specific contracts could later follow under that structural agreement. Alternatively, the parties could use this form-based mechanism each time they need a specific contract with each other. It is not fully clear under existing (non-statutory) common law that such form terms would be enforced when both sides are entirely automated, but of course American courts have been rather eager (probably too eager) to enforce standardized form terms in the general case, and there is no specific reason to think they would oppose enforcement here.

Even if form terms wouldn't be enough (apart from UETA) for software to set up entirely new agreements with other software, the law provides several other paths to permit two parties to use automation to enter into an agreement with each other without any prior structural agreement between them. One possibility is to use the contractual doctrine of *assignment.* For example, the company on one side can create large numbers of generic, assignable contracts with a third-party broker – perhaps an automated one (using a structural agreement), although that is not strictly necessary to the scheme. Subsequently, the broker can simply assign these (conventional, formally human-made) contracts in automated fashion to new contracting parties as they appear. That is, new contracting partners could request that the broker assign them a new structural contract so that they might engage, under that contract, with the company's computer program.

In other words, if software can act under existing structural agreements but faces any restrictions in creating new ones, the simple workaround is to create vast numbers of assignable agreements with a single counterparty that acts as a broker and then to arrange for these contracts to be assigned to substantive counterparties when they appear. I suspect this is more of an academic exercise than something that many commercial entities will need to do, because I don't think enforceability of automated contracts is likely to be a significant problem, but the technique shows how difficult it will be for the law to stop automated transactions even if it were inclined to do so, so long as willing parties are trying to create them and there aren't other substantive problems with the contracts (like fraud, duress, or unconscionability).

2.3 DYNAMIC AGREEMENTS

The upshot is that agreements and legal instruments in general can defer essentially their entire operation – the entire sets of rights, duties, powers, and so on that they create or regulate – to software. One possibility, as discussed above, is that software can determine when and whether offers or contracts are to be issued in the first place. Another possibility, as also outlined above, is that software can write the entire static text of a contract and then cause that contract to have legal effect.

There is an important further possibility, though: agreements and legal instruments in general can defer essentially all their operations to software by means of either very general or very complex conditions.

To understand this point, it is easiest to imagine generally intelligent software that behaves much like a human. The question to be addressed is simply how a contract might enable that AI to take legal actions, within the contract's scope, without the drafter of the contract needing to have a specific sense in advance of the types of decisions the AI will make. If the drafter does have a specific sense of the decisions that the AI will make, the contract can recognize them as simple, discrete, conditions, as suggested above: "You have a duty to buy this house for $800,000 on November 17, but only if the AI's inspection of the house returns a score greater than 92."

But suppose the drafter of the agreement has a broader goal – like hiring an AI as a manager within an organization. Interestingly, this capability for AI under an agreement or instrument falls into place relatively neatly, without much further legal complexity. It is easy enough to imagine that a company's board that seeks to hire employees by means of automated AI-based determinations could issue a corporate resolution to the following effect: "People are hired by this organization when the AI outputs 'YES' in response to the submission of their application under the following specific set of conditions." The same, of course, could apply to firing – and this may be even easier to imagine, because an employment contract could contain a provision that simply reads, "This contract is terminated when the AI produces an email to your corporate email address with the subject 'Sorry, it's not working out' and one of the following explanations in the email body: ..." or "This contract will be renewed on August 24 only if the AI outputs a score in your summer performance review above 1470." (To be clear, I don't mean to be uncritically sanguine about an AI firing humans; I discuss concerns related to this possibility in Chapter 5.)

It is equally easy to imagine the same board adopting a resolution that general, nonemployment contracts issued and approved by the AI – or financial accounts opened, or financial transactions made – have legal effect. A corporate manager, however, is in legal terms – at least, contractual terms – little more than the sum of these types of decisions. Even a CEO is there to make contracts, hire and fire people, give them instructions, set corporate strategy, and so on. Even a broad group of decisions can be handled in much the same way: with terms and conditions in agreements and other legal instruments. So the simple idea (and legal possibility) of computer-generated contractual agreements is enough to automate business decisions in the general case.

2.4 THE UNSUITABILITY OF AGENCY LAW FOR SOFTWARE

As discussed so far, it is accurate to say that algorithms, in some sense, can "act for" a legal entity. It may be tempting to draw an analogy between this sort of action and the action of a legal agent. Indeed, many have done so.[60]

As background, an *agent* is a legal person who can perform legal actions for a *principal*.[61] For example, in nearly all mature legal systems, entering a contract requires each party to assent to the terms of the

---

[60] *E.g.*, Scherer, *supra* note 29, at 285–90; sources cited *supra* note 25; Lehman-Wilzig, *supra* note 29, at 451–52.

[61] *Cf.* RESTATEMENT (THIRD) OF AGENCY § 1.01 (defining the legal concept of "agency"). Importantly, under the common law, only legal persons may act as legal agents. *See, e.g., id.* § 1.04 cmt. e ("To be capable of acting as a principal or an agent, it is necessary to be a person, which in this respect requires capacity to be the holder of legal rights and the object of legal duties.").

contract, but the parties do not need to express such assent themselves; they can send a representative, known as an agent, to bind them legally. Agency can be quite formal, arising from a "power of attorney" document that lists specific powers and the conditions under which they can be exercised. It can also be quite informal, leading to legal cases in which a nephew briefly helping an uncle wash his car can produce legal consequences for the uncle.[62] American law schools traditionally taught the common law of agency as a required part of the first-year curriculum, along with, for example, courses on torts, contracts, property, and crimes. But the subject is rarely taught as a freestanding subject anymore; it is often compressed into a week or less of a course on business law. Still, the American Law Institute has produced and continued to update *Restatement of the Law* treatises on the subject of legal agency, and many of agency law's rules are rich and debatable in the same manner as rules about contract law and tort law.

There appears to be a drive to make use of this body of law to accommodate the actions of algorithms. Algorithms may seem to act for a company just as a human agent would. But extending agency law in this way is likely to lead to confusion because the legal subject of agency has a poor conceptual and functional fit with algorithms. Essentially, while the casual metaphor of "electronic agent" makes sense in a variety of casual contexts, the analogy between algorithm and legal agent breaks down because of many structures and details within agency law.

Using agency law to integrate algorithms into the law has several specific drawbacks. First, it needlessly complicates the law's response to unexpected action by algorithms; the law of agency has sensitive rules, which rest on various parties' knowledge, intent, and reasonableness, in order to assign liability among principals, agents, and third parties, and these rules do not neatly or helpfully address the problems of algorithms. (It would be better to let the law of contracts govern gaps in agreements raised by unexpected algorithmic action.) Second, relatedly, it introduces novel ambiguities, which agency law is ill-equipped to address, about who the principal is for the action of algorithms. (By contrast, an agreement that recognizes an algorithm's verifiable state

---

[62] *See, e.g.*, Heims v. Hanke, 93 N.W.2d 455 (Wis. 1958).

raises no such ambiguity.) Third, agency law's significant rules about the liability of agents – which provide important protections to principals and third parties – would have no place in a legal regime that did not recognize the legal personhood of algorithmic agents. (It would be better simply to let normal principles of tort law apply to legal persons who put algorithmic processes in motion.) In short, the law of agency is a poor fit as a candidate for a legal technique to accommodate algorithms, and the *Restatement (Third) of Agency* is correct to require that legal agents be legal persons.[63] Instead, as described above, recognizing algorithms as providing potentially relevant conditions for legal agreements and other instruments shows more promise as a way to permit businesses and individuals to give algorithms the legal effects they intend for them to have.

The rest of this section will consider in more detail the objections I have just outlined. By highlighting problems with using agency law to recognize the action of software, this section's goal is to demonstrate further that agreements are a sounder approach. Attention to these problems is needed because agency principles appear to have become the leading contender for how autonomous or intelligent software should fit into the law.

2.4.1 The Ambiguities of Agency Law As Applied to Algorithmic Agents

Agency law is widely misunderstood; traditionally it was complicated by excessive categorization of the actions of agents, particularly into different types of authority treated as "express," "implied," "inherent," and so on. The *Restatement (Third) of Agency* is a significant improvement over classical legal conceptions of the subject, providing unifying rules that eliminate unnecessary categories. Perhaps the core principle governing agents is the notion of "actual authority" – that is, whether an agent has been empowered by a principal to enter contracts

---

[63] *See* RESTATEMENT (THIRD) OF AGENCY § 1.04 cmt. e. While agents must be legal persons, they do not necessarily need to have capacity to contract in their own right. *Id.* § 3.05 cmt. b ("It is not necessary for an agent, as to the action taken, to have capacity to hold legal rights or be subject to liabilities."). So, for example, a child or a legally incompetent adult could still be an agent.

or perform other binding legal actions on behalf of the principal. The *Restatement (Third)* expresses a simple, unified rule for the existence of such actual authority: "Actual authority ... is created by a principal's manifestation to an agent that, as reasonably understood by the agent, expresses the principal's assent that the agent take action on the principal's behalf."[64]

That simple rule shows, on its own, one of the most significant problems with an attempt to use agency law to harmonize the law's treatment of algorithms: the core determination of the power of an agent is based on what is "reasonably understood by the agent" and so requires of candidate agents that we be able to characterize their understanding as reasonable or not. While it is possible that sufficiently advanced algorithms can be judged in this way, there is no current legal standard, and no obviously productive candidate for a legal standard, that would judge today's algorithms based on what they could reasonably have understood their purported principals to mean. Because classical terminology and categorization obscured this underlying determination of reasonableness, it may not have been evident to commentators that it is difficult for the common law of agency even to get off the ground without agents whose behavior can be judged in human terms. For example, Scherer, in his recent analysis of different legal analogies that might apply to autonomous systems, does not address this problem.[65] Chopra and White address it with reference to the classical categories of agency law, essentially arguing that algorithms might have "actual express authority" but not "actual implied authority,"[66] but they appear to believe that the determination of "actual express authority" will be straightforward whereas, in the real world, it is unlikely to be: it still depends on judging the principal's communications from the perspective of a reasonable agent.[67] Actual

---

[64] *Id.* § 3.01.

[65] See Scherer, *supra* note 29.

[66] *See* Chopra & White, *supra* note 25.

[67] Chopra and White's 2011 book is similar. Their analysis is extensive and sophisticated, laying out, for example, the theoretical economic effects of allocating risk among the various parties to a transaction formed by an electronic agent – organized by the classical categories of agency. *See* CHOPRA & WHITE, *supra* note 25, at 40–61. But they appear to believe the complications in real-world application are less significant than I believe them to be; for example, as to "actual express authority," they write:

authority is trivially easy to analyze when the subjective intent of the principal, the subjective understanding of the agent (if it has one), and the reasonable understanding of both all line up similarly. But when these three possible understandings of the principal's instructions depart from one another, it is only the rich, contextual, human rules of agency law that can break the tie.

For example, suppose a company uses an algorithm to negotiate with contractual counterparties. (This might involve anything from a simple website that posts prices to a complex algorithmic broker of contracts or financial trades.) The algorithm, in some details of its operation, departs slightly from the principal's understanding of what was possible. The counterparty's software takes advantage of this drift. The normal rules of agency law are unhelpful here. As to actual authority, they would ask whether the algorithm reasonably understood the principal's instructions – a meaningless question.

How, then, is the law to determine whether an algorithm properly binds a principal? The core rule of agency law provides no answer. Perhaps other rules of agency law, like the rules governing apparent authority, provide some useful guidance, but as I will describe later these rules raise other problems that suggest they are ill-suited to help the law recognize algorithms.

By contrast, this problem doesn't arise if we treat the legal effects of algorithms as arising simply from agreements. Of course, there can still be significant dispute over the meaning of an agreement and whether it covers unexpected conduct by an algorithm, but that sort of dispute and ambiguity are conventional legal questions concerning the interpretation

> Where an agent has actual authority to enter a contract, the principal is liable, whether or not the principal would have entered that contract if he or she had had the opportunity to review it. Here, the principal is the least-cost avoider of the risk of entering an unwanted contract, since it is better placed than the third party to know its preferences, and can easily instruct the agent about its wishes. There is no material difference between the case of a human and artificial agent that would motivate a different conclusion in this class of cases.

Id. at 51. I don't think this type of analysis is sufficient to determine the existence or scope of software's agency powers in difficult cases, because actual authority is defined in terms of how a reasonable agent would process the principal's instructions at the time the agent acts.

of legal instruments. Thus, if an organization has an operating agreement purporting to assign particular legal effects to the verifiable state of an algorithm and the algorithm behaves in an unexpected fashion, the law associated with the interpretation of business entities' operating agreements can address this problem in the way it addresses any other problem. If a plain-meaning rule applies to limit the interpretation of a textual agreement, courts can use that rule; to the extent any party's subjective intent is important, the law would look to the intent of whoever drafted the operating agreement; and the law might develop doctrines that govern unexpected circumstances, as it has done in the doctrines of impossibility, impracticability, and so on. My argument is not that no legal questions are possible when agreements recognize algorithms, just that we already have techniques for addressing those problems, and there are established practical and academic debates that accommodate the important policies and differences in judgment among legal experts as to the resolution of those problems. Nothing similar exists if we look to the law of agency to try to resolve the same sort of ambiguity.

Moreover, using agreements to give legal effects to algorithms allows the law to be agnostic with regard to the capabilities or other characteristics of the algorithms. We do not need algorithms to be sufficiently advanced that they could be judged as being reasonable or unreasonable in human terms. We can avoid relying on expert understanding of just what a neural net "thought" it saw. Instead, the law's focus remains where it should be: on the intent, and the expression of that intent, by those who decided to give legal effects to algorithms by means of adopting agreements or other legal instruments.

2.4.2 The Ambiguous Principals of Algorithmic Agents

A closely related problem is that without an agreement to recognize the legal significance of an algorithm's operation, it is unclear who the principal is.[68] That is, if we model algorithms as agents, it is unclear in the general case who they are agents for. In many practical settings,

---

[68] Note that the existence of an agency relationship does not require the existence of a contract. *See* RESTATEMENT (THIRD) OF AGENCY § 1.01 cmt. d. ("[T]he consensual aspect of agency does not mean that an enforceable contract underlies or accompanies each relation of agency.").

there are many existing individuals or businesses that have a role in developing and executing algorithms. These include the designer(s) of the algorithm who specify its needs and its business role; the programmer(s) who write the software that makes up the algorithm; those who choose to run the algorithm in a particular context; the owners or possessors of the hardware on which the algorithm is executed;[69] the owners or possessors of the physical space in which the algorithms are executed; those who own part or all of the intellectual property associated with the algorithm; those who own, control, or have rights to process or restrict processing of part or all of the data that the algorithm uses; and all of the possible legal principals of any of these parties. In certain contexts, our instincts can be relatively clear about whom an algorithm is "acting" for; for example, nobody would seriously think the developer of customizable, off-the-shelf software for pricing merchandise was itself intending to make offers to sell specific merchandise merely because a retail website used the algorithm that the developer created and supplied. But one lesson of the common law is that nuances are difficult to predict across novel contexts – and often even across familiar contexts. The choice of one or several legal principals for an algorithm's action almost certainly should depend on the intent and reasonable understanding of the various parties involved in the creation and use of the algorithm, their prior dealings with one another, and so on.

Agency law gives us little guidance about such matters. Essentially, saying that software is someone's "agent" just states an assumption about how the principal should be chosen; it does not justify that choice. By contrast, the agreements of the parties give us significant guidance about such matters. What is a potentially complex choice-of-principal question under agency law is very simple if we choose to recognize algorithms where agreements recognize them; the rule is then simply that a legal person is bound contractually by the action of an algorithm when that person's agreements contain conditions that depend on the verifiable state of the algorithm.

When others have addressed the problem of algorithms' ambiguous or multiple principals, they have done so primarily for the purposes of tort

---

[69] Of course, today the "hardware" may be virtual, in which case the problems are multiplied.

liability.[70] I believe this is asking agency law to do too much, and it may also rest on a common conceptual confusion about agency law. In general, principals are *not* liable for the torts of their agents merely because of the agency relationship; there is a special category of agents known today simply as employees[71] who give rise to vicarious liability for principals in *respondeat superior*.[72] The definition of "employee" in this context is ambiguous and disputed, but probably the most important characteristic of an employee is that the principal have the right to control not just the employee's output but also the manner of the employee's processing.[73] This criterion translates very badly to algorithms, particularly as machine learning makes it more difficult for anyone to explain or control the details of an algorithm's internal processing. Even without the complexity of machine learning, however, legal classification here is likely to be both difficult and unhelpful. For example, if *A* buys a commercial software package from *B* and *B* allows *A* to configure the software only in particular ways but then *A* puts the algorithm into wide practice and injuries result, it is hard to classify the algorithm as *A*'s employee under traditional principle of agency law: *A* does not control the internal operation of the algorithm. But *A*'s knowing, widescale use of the algorithm may well have been unreasonable. To address this situation legally, it is much simpler to let conventional principles of tort law apply: *A* and *B* should be liable, individually and/or jointly, based on whether either of them has acted unreasonably in failing to prevent the injuries that have resulted. Agency law seems to add nothing helpful – and it is unnecessary to look to agency law to reach a wrongful party, as tort law is already sufficient.[74] Almost

---

[70] *E.g.*, Scherer, *supra* note 29, at 287 ("Under agency law, an agent can have multiple principals, either by being the agent of another agent ... or by being the agent of two or more co-principals. Each principal can be held responsible for the agent's tortious acts, as long as those acts are otherwise within the scope of the agency. In the context of A.I. systems, this structure expands the range of potential sources of compensation if an A.I. system causes harm ... .").

[71] This historical term in the common law of agency was "servants."

[72] For an overview of the doctrine of *respondeat superior*, see SHAWN BAYERN, CLOSELY HELD ORGANIZATIONS 51–88 (2d ed. 2020).

[73] *See id.* at 53–54.

[74] There is a class of torts that traditionally has been tied closely to agency law but seems to depart little, or not at all, from ordinary principles of tort liability. For example, RESTATEMENT (THIRD) OF AGENCY § 7.05 provides that "A principal who conducts an activity through an agent is subject to liability for harm to a third party caused by the agent's conduct if the harm was caused by the principal's negligence in selecting, training,

certainly, at least today, very little will be added to the law by an effort to differentiate between algorithms that are employees and algorithms that are independent contractors! But that is precisely what would be necessary, in the general case, for agency law to be useful in assigning vicarious tort liability to those who create or make use of algorithms.

It may be worth adding that my goal is not simply to defend the law's conventional treatment of algorithms and the people associated with them. For example, the difficulty of assigning responsibility to one or more people involved with an algorithm exists under the *Restatement (Third)*'s view of algorithms as instrumentalities, just as it does for a view of algorithms as agents. Recognizing the role of agreements – whether in determining the effects of an instrumentality or even in determining who is or isn't an agent – appears to be the best way out of murkiness. To put it differently, we probably can recognize that program X is the instrumentality or agent of business Y only by recognizing at least an implicit agreement (on the part of Y and its potential contractual counterparties) that X will serve that role. The law will do better to pay more attention to such agreements, particularly as they become more express and more complex, rather than to take them for granted or make generic assumptions about their content.

2.4.3 The Complexity of Liability in Agency Law

Agency law is a rich part of the common law designed to allocate liability sensitively among principals, agents, and third parties. Its scheme collapses if purported agents are unable to bear liability because they are not legal persons.

For example, consider a problem similar to the general one described above: a business makes use of an algorithm to enter into contracts with third parties, and the algorithm behaves unexpectedly and causes the business to appear to enter contracts that it had no desire to enter. (This could be anything from transient mispricing on an automated website to a complex, hard-to-detect error in the algorithm's determination of

---

retaining, supervising, or otherwise controlling the agent." In that case, however, the principal's own negligence (in selecting, training, etc.) the agent is sufficient for tort liability; as I have described in more detail in BAYERN, *supra* note 72, at 82–88, no new principle of agency law is needed to explain this rule.

which third parties to contract with.) As I pointed out, agency law's rules concerning actual authority are ill-suited to address this type of unexpected processing precisely because they depend on an evaluation of the reasonableness of the purported agent.

Perhaps the ambiguity might be resolved not by rules of "actual" authority but what in the United States is called "apparent" authority (and is elsewhere commonly called "ostensible" authority). These rules, designed mainly for the protection of third parties contracting with a principal through an agent, effectively deem that a purported agent has authority to bind the principal as long as the third party reasonably believes, based on the principal's manifestations to that third party, that the agent had the authority to act for the principal even if the agent lacked that (actual) authority. Because apparent authority depends only on the reasonableness of the third party and the facts concerning the principal's manifestations to it, it seems like an adaptive enough way to allocate responsibility between principals and third parties. But a different feature of agency law shows why this principle, too, maps badly onto algorithms: when an agent acts with apparent but not actual authority – which is to say, when the agent has acted unreasonably, but the third party has not – the agent is liable to the principal for harms caused by the agent's assumption of nondelegated authority. Moreover, agents are understood to make a warranty of authority to third parties, effectively representing that if they are purporting to act for a principal, they have the authority to do so; third parties may sue purported agents for harms that result from the breaches of that implied warranty.[75] This too makes little sense for agents that cannot bear liability because they are not legal persons.

All these rules exhibit a balance designed to protect reasonable parties at the expense of unreasonable ones. The balance does not exist when the agent is not a legal person, and the resulting set of rules is in some sense not actually "agency law" but an arbitrary subset of it. That doesn't mean the resulting set of rules is necessarily wrong, only that the use of an analogy to agency law is incomplete and suspect – and that the results need to be defended independently on functional grounds. To put it differently, agency law currently functions as

---

[75] *See* RESTATEMENT (THIRD) OF AGENCY § 6.10.

a system, and paying attention to only part of that system may lead to problematic consequences.

In short, analogizing algorithms to agents is popular rhetorically, but agency law is not a functional mechanism for incorporating algorithms into law. Instead, recognizing that agreements of any form can give legal effect to the verifiable state of algorithms provides an extremely flexible mechanism for connecting algorithms to existing law, and it lays the foundation for the discussion in the next chapter, which shows that agreements can go as far as to enable algorithms to act autonomously under existing law.

3   IN THE COMPANY OF ROBOTS

The Creation of Autonomous Organizations

Since the 1980s, a quiet revolution has taken place in modern American *organizational law*, a term I use to refer to the law covering the internal governance of organizations, such as corporations, limited liability companies (LLCs), partnerships, and nonprofits. New forms of organizational entities, like the LLC, resemble familiar business organizations, but they differ radically in largely unrecognized ways – generally because of their extreme flexibility and adaptability.

This chapter highlights the ability of new organizations, particularly the LLC, to serve as legal "containers" for autonomous systems like computer programs or robots. Put simply, LLCs and probably other modern American business forms are flexible enough to permit a phenomenon that most commentators have traditionally considered impossible: effective legal status (or "legal personhood") for nonhuman agents without fundamental legal reform. Because of the unrecognized capabilities of modern entities, anything from a dog to a computer program, or from a 12-year-old child to a robot, can functionally participate in the legal system – buying and selling property, suing and being sued, and so forth. The resulting entity is functionally autonomous. To be clear, it is not immune from legal regulation; like any LLC, it is subject to statutes, regulations, administrative oversight, and civil and criminal process. But as a matter of internal governance, the entities that the techniques described in this chapter can create are meaningfully autonomous: they can exist perpetually and be governed only by software, not by the ongoing influence of individual human owners.

3.1 BACKGROUND: LEGAL PERSONHOOD AS "LEGAL TECHNOLOGY"

At the outset, some preliminary discussion will be helpful. For the purposes of this discussion, as I noted in Chapter 1, *legal personhood* is simply the capacity of a person, system, or legal entity to be recognized by law sufficiently to perform basic legal functions. As I define the term, it refers to the ability to participate in the fundamental relationships regulated by the private law – such as the capability to own property, enter a contract, file a lawsuit, be named in a lawsuit, serve as a legal principal, and serve as a legal agent. My use of the notion of legal personhood matches its understanding in the private law. Importantly, in this context it is a neutral term with respect to many broader political rights. Recently, at least within American political discussion, a broader concept of legal personhood has become politically and rhetorically contentious; for example, the term arises in debates over whether corporate entities have constitutional rights to freedom of speech or to participation in the electoral process.[76] This book avoids that particular political debate; private-law personhood is not logically tied to constitutional protections – any more than it is tied, for example, to the right of two natural persons to marry[77] – and this book takes no position concerning the scope of American or other countries' constitutional rights.

As a matter of positive law, of course, legal or juristic "personality" is reserved for natural persons and specific types of legal entities, such as corporations, in modern legal systems. Other physical systems – such as (1) nonhuman forms of life, including other animals; (2) natural systems; and (3) algorithmic processes implemented in

---

[76] *See* Elizabeth Pollman, *Reconceiving Corporate Personhood*, 2011 UTAH L. REV. 1629, 1629–32 (discussing a similar distinction in the meaning of corporate personhood and applying it to modern debates about constitutional rights). For a discussion of different functions of corporate personhood generally, see Margaret M. Blair, *Corporate Personhood and the Corporate Persona*, 2013 U. ILL. L. REV. 785; *see also* ERIC W. ORTS, BUSINESS PERSONS: A LEGAL THEORY OF THE FIRM (2013).

[77] Of course, nobody thinks two corporations can get married, though they can merge. (Conversely, nobody thinks two natural persons can merge.) Despite the inability to marry, corporations are undisputedly legal persons in the realm of private law and organizational law; at least as a matter of current law, nobody questions the ability of a corporation to enter into a contract or open a bank account.

software or hardware, including those that underlie modern computer systems – are not traditionally treated as legal persons. Accordingly, even if such systems, to varying degrees, could be said to make decisions autonomously, their acts are normally understood to have a different legal nature from the acts of natural persons. For example, as discussed in the previous chapter, at least in the United States a computer program cannot presently serve formally as a legal agent, simply because it formally lacks legal personhood,[78] and even if it would be commercially, politically, or socially useful for the computer program to have a similar capability. (Chapter 2 demonstrated a few ways to work around this restriction, so that in practice a computer program can, today, taken on the *functions* of a legal person. For example, it can enter a willing party into a contract as long as the principal uses the techniques of Chapter 2 to set up the software appropriately.)

A surprising implication of modern American business-entity law has the potential to reform more broadly this limitation in the legal treatment of algorithms. The rise of a relatively new organizational form known as the limited liability company (LLC) – which has emphasized the freedom of those involved in the organization to determine its internal structure and, accordingly, has permitted forms of governance much more flexible than those in traditional partnerships or corporations – provides one possible conceptual framework for adapting the private law to technological innovations. Specifically, modern LLC statutes in the United States permit the development of "memberless" legal entities – that is, legal persons whose actions are determined solely by agreement or algorithm, not in any ongoing fashion by human members or owners. Such autonomous legal entities are a strong candidate for a legal "technology" or technique to respond to innovations in autonomous systems.

It is sometimes helpful to treat legal mechanisms as technologies, reinforcing the previous chapter's discussion of a sort of isomorphism between software and legal instruments. Nicholas Murray Butler, the president of Columbia University for most of the early 1900s, expressed a similar point more enthusiastically at the Annual Banquet of the New York Chamber of Commerce in 1911:

---

[78] *See* RESTATEMENT (THIRD) OF AGENCY § 1.04 cmt. e.

I weigh my words, when I say that in my judgment the limited liability corporation[79] is the greatest single discovery of modern times, whether you judge it by its social, by its ethical, by its industrial, or, in the long run, – after we understand it and know how to use it, – by its political, effects. Even steam and electricity are far less important than the limited liability corporation, and they would be reduced to comparative impotence without it.[80]

Butler went on to describe the corporation as a necessary "engine for carrying on international trade on a scale commensurate with modern needs and opportunities." To be clear, I don't endorse Butler's sentiment, just his view that it is possible to think of legal-organizational structures as innovations, much like technological advances.

Memberless entities, such as those that modern LLC statutes support (even if unintentionally), constitute a similar innovation in their ability to accommodate software flexibly and adaptively. Such memberless entities can encapsulate a physically autonomous system and provide a mechanism for that system to take legally autonomous action. Organizational law, as it often does, thus provides a connection or interface between a system (on one hand) and the various bodies of rules in private law, such as contract, tort, and property (on the other).[81]

In short, just as a business corporation is an opportunity to represent a complex social system (one that involves humans, software, and other instrumentalities) as a legal person, memberless legal entities may be a suitable legal response to physical systems that operate

---

[79] Butler was referring just to what we would call the corporation. "Limited liability" – which is to say, no liability for participants arising only from their participation in the corporation – is a feature of business corporations. The "limited liability company" or LLC did not appear in US statutes until 1977. It bears mentioning that the term "limited liability" is somewhat imprecise; it is often described by noting that the "liability" of those who invest in a corporation is "limited" to their investment. That description does not apply the legal notion of liability correctly, however. The investors' *loss* is limited to their investment; they face *no* liability for the activities of the corporation. *See* BAYERN, *supra* note 72, at 182–83 (discussing MELVIN ARON EISENBERG & JAMES D. COX, CORPORATIONS AND OTHER BUSINESS ORGANIZATIONS 415 (10th ed. 2011)).

    Others have used the term "legal technology" to refer to business entities. *See, e.g.*, LAWRENCE M. FRIEDMAN, A HISTORY OF AMERICAN LAW 496 (4th ed. 2019).

[80] NEW YORK CHAMBER OF COMMERCE, ANNUAL BANQUET OF THE CHAMBER OF COMMERCE OF THE STATE OF NEW YORK 47 (Press of the Chamber of Commerce 1911).

[81] BAYERN, *supra* note 72, at 104 (describing ways in which organizational law serves as an interface between other areas of private law).

independently, in an ongoing way, from human intervention. On this view, the precise degree of autonomy of a system does not directly dictate the law's response to it; instead, a machine's legal autonomy – or indeed the legal autonomy of any algorithm, process, or system – can derive simply from the power people have under existing law to create artificial legal entities for more traditional purposes.

As I will discuss later in more detail, there are reasons to think using memberless LLCs to give personhood to autonomous software is a more adaptive approach than its alternatives. In particular, a regime that relies solely on public bodies (like legislatures) to grant legal-entity status may react too slowly to technological change, and it may raise questions about precise degrees of autonomy that the law is currently ill-equipped to answer. A regime that refuses to recognize autonomous systems at all may, similarly, limit the social potential of such systems – or drive them underground or ensure that the law poorly captures the functional relationships associated with them. And there is reason to think that even the arbitrary, rapid proliferation of legal entities causes little harm, either for legal processes or for the goals that law intends to serve; for example, in several legal jurisdictions within the United States, a concept known as the "series LLC" has begun to permit individuals or existing organizations to create multitudes of separate LLCs without even requiring registration of the new individual entities with the government.[82] In short, given that the legal system already has legally recognized entities like corporations and harmonized that recognition with other areas of law, recognizing and harmonizing autonomous software may prove to be an easier challenge than commentators typically assume.

One final note before proceeding: in referring to autonomous systems or autonomous software, I mean to do so broadly. The chapter's conclusions are applicable to many different types of systems. On one end of the spectrum, an "autonomous system" might be a fairly mundane, conventional program that performs a defined role, such as a network of computer processes that operates vending machines that accept cryptocurrency (or some other online payment that requires no specific interface with the legal recognition or titling of bank

---

[82] *See* DEL. LTD. LIAB. CO. ACT. § 18–215.

accounts).[83] On the other, it might – in the future – be an intelligent robot that passes the Turing Test.[84] It can be anything from a relatively simple distributed system that coordinates human activity (like votes or payments) to an independent and adaptive intelligent system. Again, I take no predictive position here on the advent of various types of software-based intelligence; little of my legal discussion depends on specific attributes or capabilities of autonomous systems themselves. Indeed, just as a corporation needn't be intelligent or conscious for the legal system to recognize it, a software system needn't have these attributes to achieve legal personhood or its functional equivalent.

3.2 THE NOVELTY OF MODERN ENTITIES IN ENABLING NONHUMAN AUTONOMOUS SYSTEMS

To understand the subtly revolutionary capacities of modern organizational forms, it will be useful to consider why it was impossible for traditional organizational entities, like the classic corporation, to encapsulate and give legal life to an autonomous system.

Historically, the prototypical business *entity* is a corporation; the common law has long permitted businesses to be organized in noncorporate forms, but it was only relatively recently that it conceived those forms as legal entities or legal persons. Originally, governments chartered corporations for particular, narrow purposes; the standard example is the construction of a bridge.[85] Unlike their modern descendants, these narrowly tailored corporations could not enter a new line of

---

[83] For more discussion of this type of autonomous entity, see Shawn Bayern, *Of Bitcoins, Independently Wealthy Software, and the Zero-Member LLC*, 108 Nw. U. L. Rev. 1485, 1486 (2014) ("Bitcoin allows autonomously operating software – such as a computer virus or the software that manages a network of vending machines – to exercise control over significant wealth, not as an intermediary for individuals or companies, but rather, in a functionally meaningful sense, in its own right.").

[84] *See* A. M. Turing, *Computing Machinery and Intelligence*, 59 Mind 433 (1950) (proposing that a functional answer to the question "Can machines think?" be determined through an "imitation game" in which a computer seeks to impersonate a human in written correspondence).

[85] The prominence of the bridge-building example in American commentary may date to Charles River Bridge v. Warren Bridge, 36 U.S. 420, 420 (1837) (involving "a corporation created by an act of the legislature of the state of Massachusetts, passed on the 9th of March, 1785, entitled 'An act for incorporating certain persons for the purpose of building

business or even adapt to many changing business circumstances; the doctrine of *ultra vires* ("beyond its powers") could invalidate corporate actions that overstepped a corporation's original charter.[86] For example, a bridge-building corporation could not open a general retail store at the foot of the bridge.

Clearly, the narrowly focused historical form of the corporation does little to aid an autonomous system that seeks legal personhood. Getting a modern government to issue a personalized charter is likely to prove as difficult as getting a modern government to recognize an individual autonomous system outright as a legal person. But corporations, at least as they have been conceived traditionally, impose other limitations that are just as significant for our purposes as the limitations in a charter, and these limitations remained significant even as the power of corporations to conduct general business expanded and corporations became allowed to exercise "any lawful business" (as opposed to building a specific bridge).

For example, one specific restriction in the historical corporate form is that the corporation be managed (or at least overseen)[87] by a board of directors and that this board be populated by *natural* persons (the law's term for individuals). Thus, for example, the Delaware General Corporation Law provides simply: "The board of directors of a corporation shall consist of 1 or more members, each of whom shall be a natural person."[88] This restriction is standard across American law.[89] The requirement that directors be natural persons historically ruled out a corporation or a partnership from serving as a director, probably in the interest of clarity in decision making and of corporate structure. (If a general partnership were a member of a corporate

---

a bridge over Charles river, between Boston and Charlestown, and supporting the same during forty years.'").

[86] *See* BAYERN, *supra* note 72, at 223–24.

[87] *See* Melvin Aron Eisenberg, *Legal Models of Management Structure in the Modern Corporation: Officers, Directors, and Accountants*, 63 CAL. L. REV. 375, 376 (1975) ("Instead [of a managerial board], in small, closely-held corporations the business is typically managed directly by owner-managers, while in large, publicly-held corporations . . . the business is typically managed by the top executives.").

[88] DEL. GEN. CORP. L. § 141(b).

[89] *E.g.*, MODEL BUS. CORP. ACT § 8.03(a) (2016 rev.) (updated through Dec. 2020) [hereinafter MBCA] ("A board of directors shall consist of one or more individuals . . . ."); *id.* § 1.40 ("'Individual' means a natural person.").

board, the law of corporations would need rules about what to do if the general partnership dissolved or if the partners disagreed and dead-locked.) Clearly, of course, this requirement would have made it impossible to create an autonomous corporation – that is, one that does not require an ongoing association with any natural persons.

Starting around the mid-1900s, corporate law became more flexible in terms of the permissible underlying structures of corporations.[90] To address the needs of closely held corporations – "ranging from family businesses to joint ventures owned by large public corporations"[91] – courts began to permit unanimous shareholders to restrict a corporation's board of directors severely, substituting a flexible, sta-tutorily unspecified governance by private agreement.[92] Eventually, state statutes came to give more explicit power to unanimous share-holders, and the Model Business Corporation Act – the model for many US states' corporation statutes – eventually went so far as to uphold unanimous shareholder agreements "even [if they are] inconsistent with ... this Act in that [they] ... eliminate[] the board of directors."[93]

The modern Model Business Corporation Act, then, comes very close to enabling an autonomous system to inhabit a corporation and use the corporation as its interface to the legal system. To see why this is so, recall Chapter 2's discussion: a legally enforceable agreement may give legal significance to any features of the verifiable state of any process (such as an algorithm or physical system) by specifying legal conditions satisfied by features of that state. As an example, a simple bilateral contract may make an obligation conditional on the output of a computer program, the behavior of a dog, and so on. The principle that an algorithm and an agreement can correspond to one another takes this example a step further: it recognizes that a sufficiently broad agreement can allow essentially unlimited legal influence for an algo-rithm. Consider, for example, an artificially intelligent algorithm that passes the Turing Test in apparently acting roughly as a human acts.[94] An agreement can, by specifying obligations and conditions, effectively

---

[90] *See id.* § 7.32 cmt.
[91] *Id.*
[92] *See id.*
[93] *Id.* § 7.32(a).
[94] *See supra* note 84.

delegate legal rights and decision-making powers to such an algorithm even though that algorithm is not a legal person. An agreement might say, for example, "Your obligation to perform is discharged if the algorithm indicates X," where X could be (for an unsophisticated algorithm) a formal output on a computer terminal or (for an artificially intelligent algorithm) something that approaches a description of human understanding and action (like "that it expresses satisfaction with the arrangement and physically signs a release form").

To apply this principle to the foregoing discussion of corporate structure, suppose that a natural person E (for *enabler*) forms corporation C, signing an "agreement"[95] that specifies that C is to have no board of directors and instead shall take all legal actions determined by A (an autonomous system). In this scenario, A can seem to use the corporation for its own legal purposes, whatever they may be. This explains how a modern closely held corporation can permit an autonomous system to *approach* something like legal personhood. Still, C is not truly an autonomous legal entity, for E remains a shareholder and can continue to exert control over the entity.[96] And there is little that any of the parties involved (E, A, or C) can apparently do to retire the corporation's shares entirely. E can of course transfer the shares – some or all of them – to a new shareholder, but corporate law still appears to impose a requirement that there be at least one shareholder.[97] And shareholders must be legal persons.[98] The result is apparently that even in a modern corporation with a shareholder agreement that eliminates the board of directors, ultimate authority in the corporation must rest

---

[95] The term "shareholder agreement" as used in the Model Business Corporation Act appears to cover single-party operating agreements; at least, nothing in the Act equates "agreement" with "contract" or requires the assent of two or more parties. Even if such a requirement existed, however, it would not change much of the discussion in the text.

[96] Though the Model Business Corporation Act is not fully clear on this point, if E is the sole founding shareholder and remains the sole shareholder, E probably can revoke the operating agreement. *See* MBCA § 7.32(b) ("An agreement authorized by this section shall be ... subject to amendment only by all persons who are shareholders at the time of the amendment, unless the agreement provides otherwise.").

[97] *Id.* § 6.01(b) ("The articles of incorporation must authorize ... one or more classes or series of shares that together have full voting rights ....."). Note that § 7.32(a) of the Act does not include eliminating the notion of shareholders from its list of the capabilities of an enforceable shareholder agreement.

[98] *E.g.*, *id.* § 1.40 (defining "shareholder" as "the *person* in whose name shares are registered") (emphasis added).

with an existing legal person who has at least some type of share in the corporation.[99] Accordingly, while for practical purposes a modern corporation could serve as a convenient way to permit an autonomous system to act as roughly a legal person for a while, any arrangement would depend on the ongoing consent of an existing private party.[100]

Of course, traditional common law permitted forms of business other than corporations. Historically, the main alternative in the common law to the corporation was the general partnership. As originally conceived, and as embodied in the widely adopted Uniform Partnership Act (UPA) of 1914, general partnerships were not legal entities and did not interact significantly with the concept of legal personhood. In other words, partnerships did not have rights or duties themselves; a classical statement of the matter was that "a partnership was no more a legal entity than was a friendship."[101] A partnership could not sue or be sued; instead, the individual partners would have

---

[99] Professor LoPucki may have misread me in attributing to me the idea that the existence of board of directors, rather than the existence of a shareholder, ties modern corporations to natural persons. *See* LoPucki, *supra* note 24, at 907. As I observed in the article to which he was responding, the requirement of a board of directors may have imposed historical constraints, but under modern statutes like the Model Business Corporation Act that permit shareholders to eliminate the board of directors, the requirement of a conventional legal person as shareholder is a more significant restraint on the ability to set up formally autonomous organizations by means of the corporate form. *See* Shawn Bayern, *The Implications of Modern Business-Entity Law for the Regulation of Autonomous Systems*, 19 STAN. TECH. L. REV. 93, 99–100 (2015).

[100] Thus, earlier explorations of corporations powered by algorithms were theoretical or imaginary rather than practical. The idea has a long history as a purely imaginative matter. For example, Meir Dan-Cohen, more than thirty years ago, suggested the possibility of a self-owning company. *See* MEIR DAN-COHEN, RIGHTS, PERSONS, AND ORGANIZATIONS 46 (1986); *see also* Katsuhito Wai, *Persons, Things and Corporations: The Corporate Personality Controversy and Comparative Corporate Governance*, 47 AM. J. COMP. L. 583 (1999) (briefly describing the intellectual history of this idea and attributing it to others as well, including Martin Wolff and Alfred Conard). The oldest specific indication of the theoretical concept – just as an idea, not a workable legal artifact tied to practical ongoing control by software – that I'm aware of dates to 1915, when Max Hachenburg published *Zum Erwerbe eigener Geschäftsanteile durch die Gesellschaft mit beschränkterHaftung* ("On the Acquisition of Its Own Shares by the GmbH" – the German analogue of an LLC), in FESTSCHRIFT FOR COHN 79 (1915). For discussion of the modern German understanding of "Kein-Mann-GmbH" – zero-member LLC – entities, see Bayern, Burri, et al., *supra* note 53.

Through creative transaction engineering, the modern corporate form is probably flexible enough to sustain an autonomous organization, but the point needn't be pressed because LLCs (and other forms, like limited partnerships) are more suitable anyway.

[101] EISENBERG & COX, *supra* note 79, at 132. *Cf. supra* note 2 regarding Hohfeldian jural relations.

to file a suit or be named as defendants. The statute made complicated arrangements so that bank accounts could be titled in partnerships' names; surprisingly to common lawyers outside the United States, the UPA effectively created a novel tenurial framework – "tenancy in partnership" – to address this need.[102] Still, the partnership itself was not a legal person.

Primarily because the application of legal personhood to partnerships simplifies the rest of partnership law, the modern Uniform Partnership Act of 1997 – known commonly as the Revised Uniform Partnership Act, or RUPA – adopts a position that was argued in 1914 but did not take hold: namely, that general partnerships should be treated as legal entities – that is, as legal persons. RUPA is now the law in the vast majority of US jurisdictions. It is worthwhile to consider, then, the possibility that modern general partnerships might provide legal capabilities for autonomous systems. The proposed technique would be as follows:

(1) X and Y (two natural persons or preexisting legal entities) form a general partnership under RUPA, entering into a partnership agreement under which
   (a) the partnership adopts the decisions of A (an autonomous system);
   (b) the partnership will not dissolve upon the dissociation of the partners;
(2) X dissociates from the partnership;
(3) Y dissociates from the partnership.[103]

---

[102] UNIF. P'SHIP ACT. § 25(2)(a) (1914) (creating and defining "tenancy in partnership").

[103] A brief note may be helpful about the concept of *dissociation*, which is relatively new to organizational law. Historically, general partnerships were said to *dissolve*, at least by default, when the membership changed. This notion of dissolution had several potential meanings and could therefore be unclear, but it essentially meant that an event had occurred that would cause a business association in question to terminate – not necessarily immediately, but often irrevocably. (To be clear, the term applied to the start of a process that would culminate in the termination of a legal business *association* – not necessarily in the termination of the underlying business *activities*. For example, a new group of partners, having formed a new partnership, might take over the "business.") Purely as a matter of terminology, *dissolution* was a trigger that led to a process of *winding up* – settling the debts of the business association and so forth – followed by the legally effective *termination* of the business association, after which the business association legally ceased to exist. In this context, *winding up* means the same thing as *winding down*. For a more thorough pedagogical introduction, see BAYERN, supra note 72, at 145–80.

   Confusion about the concept of dissolution led to some terrible court opinions, which in turn led the Uniform Law Commission to clarify partnership law by promulgating

The first step is mostly unremarkable; clearly two legal persons can establish a partnership,[104] and RUPA provides an expansive scope for partnership agreements, so they can make use of the full range of techniques described in Chapter 2.[105] Notably, this scope appears to be sufficient under RUPA to permit the partnership to continue to exist following the second and third steps, for RUPA permits partnership agreements to modify the conditions on which a partnership dissolves and winds up except for particular, enumerated cases.[106] Nonetheless, there remains significant dispute about whether RUPA would permit even the second step – that is, whether a general partnership under RUPA can persist with only one partner, let alone no partners.[107] While I think it is possible for general partnerships under RUPA to encapsulate autonomous systems, I need not press the point here because modern LLCs provide even greater flexibility and are, conceptually and practically, a simpler route.[108]

what is commonly called the Revised Uniform Partnership Act [hereinafter RUPA] in the 1990s. This uniform act introduced the notion of *dissociation* to mark the departure of a member from an unincorporated business association. Dissociation might or might not lead to the dissolution of the entity, but introducing and defining a legal concept that covered the departure of a member – in isolation from the other effects of that departure – proved useful, and the concept was adopted by later statutes governing unincorporated businesses, including LLCs.

Accordingly, the dissociation of a partner from a partnership, or a member from an LLC, refers to a specific point at which the partner or member loses that status. Not all rights and duties between the partnership and the partner (or the LLC and the member) automatically terminate at that same point, and the departure may have various effects on the organization. Importantly, though, the discussion of the concept works at all only under the modern generation of organizational-law statutes; there is no use in trying to retrofit the concept of dissociation to an older partnership statute, for example. In referring to dissociation, this book always does so in the context of a particular modern business-association statute.

Corporate law does not ordinarily need the same concept because shareholders simply buy and sell shares.

[104] RUPA § 202(a) ("[T]he association of two or more persons to carry on as co-owners a business for profit forms a partnership . . . .").

[105] RUPA § 103(a) (providing that "the partnership agreement governs . . . relations among the partners as partners and between the partners and the partnership" except for a statutorily enumerated list of specific prohibitions).

[106] *See* RUPA § 103(b)(8).

[107] *See* Robert W. Hillman & Donald J. Weidner, *Partners Without Partners: The Legal Status of Single Person Partnerships*, 17 FORDHAM J. CORP. & FIN. L. 449 (2012) (presenting both sides of the debate).

[108] LLCs provide other advantages over general partnerships, such as limited liability, and if nothing else they require only one (rather than two) legal persons to establish them. The same analysis as in the text applies to limited liability partnerships (LLPs) governed by RUPA. Broadly similar analysis applies to limited partnerships governed by various

3.3 THE ZERO-MEMBER LLC

Consider, then, the following use of an LLC:

(1) An individual member creates a member-managed LLC,[109] filing the appropriate paperwork with the state and paying an appropriate (usually very small) filing fee.
(2) The individual causes the LLC, which is controlled by the sole member,[110] to enter into an operating agreement governing the conduct of the LLC that
    (a) specifies that the LLC will take actions as determined by an autonomous system, specifying terms or conditions as appropriate to achieve the autonomous system's legal goals; and
    (b) provides that the LLC will continue to exist even after the last member dissociates.
(3) The individual transfers ownership of any relevant physical apparatus of the autonomous system and any relevant intellectual property associated with the autonomous system or its components to the LLC.
(4) The individual, sole member, withdraws from the LLC, leaving the LLC without any members.

versions of the Uniform Limited Partnership Act, but there is no reason to explore limited partnerships in detail because of the rise of LLCs, which are more flexible and retain all or essentially all the advantages of limited partnerships.

That said, for robustness – particularly in view of new federal statutory developments, *see infra* notes 180–83 – it is worth pointing out that the technique described in this chapter transfers easily to the Uniform Limited Partnership Act (2001) (last amended 2013) [hereinafter ULPA]. Under the current version of ULPA, adopted in many US states, a limited partnership may terminate by default "after the dissociation of a person as a general partner" or "the passage of 90 consecutive days after the dissociation of the partnership's last limited partner," but these are both explicitly default rather than mandatory rules. ULPA § 801(a) & cmt. ("Except for Paragraphs (a)(6) and (7) [concerning judicial and administrative dissolution], this section comprises default rules."). Limited partnerships are thus suitable vehicles for autonomous organizations under ULPA; the technique is simply to set up a limited partnership with a general partner and a limited partner, then have both dissociate, under an appropriate operating agreement. Note that ULPA also authorizes the creation of limited-liability limited partnerships in addition to limited partnerships. See ULPA § 102(9).

[109] LLCs have two common organizational paths, "member-managed" and "manager-managed." *See, e.g.*, Unif. Ltd. Liab. Co. Act § 407 (2006) (last amended 2013) [hereinafter RULLCA]; Bayern, *supra* note 72, at 261–63. The technique I describe in the text can achieve similar results with both types of LLCs; I focus on member-managed LLCs for simplicity.

[110] RULLCA § 407(b) ("In a member-managed limited liability company, . . . the management and conduct of the company are vested in the members.").

The result is potentially a perpetual LLC – a new legal person – that requires no ongoing intervention from any preexisting legal person in order to maintain its status.

Because this technique is central to the creation of autonomous organizations, it is important to spell out these steps in some detail. Step one is mundane and simply involves the creation of an LLC with a single member. As I discuss in the next chapter, single-member companies were once regarded as bizarre, but today they are commonplace.[111] LLC statutes date to 1977, so they are a relatively recent phenomenon in American law overall, but they are uncontroversial in basic form. In fact, registering an LLC in most states is easier and cheaper than buying an airline ticket; in Florida, which sees several hundred thousand LLCs created each year, the process is as simple as going to the state government's embarrassingly named "sunbiz.org" website and paying $125 by credit card. The process is about as simple as applying for a new credit card and much simpler than applying for a new insurance policy. Some states require a little more process and significantly higher fees; for example, California's fee – which is framed explicitly as a tax – is at least $800. A very recent federal statute may increase the procedural requirements for registering companies somewhat, but probably not significantly for law-abiding applicants.[112]

As further background, modern LLC statutes provide two paths – two sets of what lawyers call *default rules*, as in rules that apply by default or without modification by the parties – for creating LLCs. One of these paths is for *member-managed* LLCs; the other is for *manager-managed* LLCs. The former of these categories is usually used by small businesses where the members have active control, much as in general partnerships; the latter is used where the size or nature of the business has led the parties to want to separate ownership from control, as in larger corporations. LLCs are thus flexible enough to accommodate single-member companies, small businesses with a few parties, and structures that resemble those of the largest public corporations. Indeed, as I have suggested in some previous work, it

---

[111] *See infra* note 146.
[112] *See infra* notes 180–83 and accompanying text.

seems almost silly to retain the other forms of business entity given the extreme flexibility of LLCs.[113] As the computer scientist Alan Perlis once put it ironically, "If you have a procedure with 10 parameters, you probably missed some."[114] The same principle applies here: if you have a legal system with a dozen different legal-entity forms, all of which accomplish much the same thing, you might as well redesign the system so that the most general one is the only one that remains. The law is slowly moving in that direction anyway just as a matter of private choice; for example, while Florida registered 310,854 new LLCs in 2019, it registered only 596 limited partnerships (LPs) and 151 limited liability limited partnerships (LLLPs).[115]

The second step in the transactional technique above starts mundanely as well. LLCs are governed by operating agreements that have roughly the same role as the "charter" or "articles of incorporation" in a corporation. That is, the operating agreement is an LLC's foundational, constitutional document. As described in more detail later in this section, LLC statutes permit these operating agreements to be extremely flexible in structuring LLCs. Unlike corporation statutes that (with some exceptions) expect there to be a board of directors, a constituency known as shareholders, etc., LLCs have no preordained structure: the LLC is flexible enough to accommodate a one-person organization, a small partnership, a big business, or even the structure of the US government itself! In other words, if someone wanted to set up an LLC that was managed by a legislative body with two houses, an executive officer with subordinates in quasi-independent administrative departments, and a "judiciary" to resolve disputes, LLCs would (relatively uncontroversially) be up to the task. Moreover, a single member of an LLC is easily permitted to set the initial operating agreement for the LLC.[116]

---

[113] *Cf.* Shawn Bayern, *Three Problems (And Two Solutions) in the Law of Partnership Formation*, 49 U. Mich. J.L. Ref. 605, 626 (2016) (suggesting "that modern American law currently lacks a principled system for vicarious business liability").

[114] Perlis, *supra* note 31.

[115] Admittedly, it still registered 95,771 for-profit corporations and 13,248 nonprofit corporations, two types of organizations that could both be subsumed by the LLC form. This is why I suggest in the text that the movement is "slow."

[116] *E.g.*, RULLCA § 106(c) ("One person intending to become the initial member of a limited liability company may assent to terms providing that upon the formation of the company the terms will become the operating agreement."). Note that, in principle

The operating agreement that the second step above calls for has two important novel provisions, however. The first places a software system "in charge" of the LLC. As discussed in Chapter 2, this involves simply writing the operating agreement to have appropriate terms and conditions to enable the software to act. A general statement is probably sufficient: "This LLC will enter into contracts and make internal governance decisions based on directions issued by" a particular software program. It would probably be prudent, at least until operating agreements like this become more commonplace, for the operating agreement to spell out as many specific conditions and capabilities of the software as possible, just for the avoidance of doubt. To a computer programmer, this is like extra error checking that is likely unnecessary; to a lawyer, it is why contracts are often twenty pages longer than they need to be. But there's no reason for a diligent drafter of an operating agreement not to include as many specific conditions they can think of, just to reduce as much as possible the opportunities for interpretive doubt. For example, the operating agreement might include clauses like the following:

- "Under this agreement, contractual offers issued to third parties by the governing software are binding on the LLC."
- "Under this agreement, this LLC accepts and ratifies any offers of contracts that are approved by the governing software under the following procedures . . . ."
- "Under this agreement, any legal notice or notifications called for by contracts of which the LLC is a party may be sent in an authenticated manner by the governing software. Such communications are binding on the LLC."
- "Under this agreement, this LLC hires employees, under the employment contract listed in Appendix A to this agreement, when the employee signs that contract and when the governing software approves it by causing an authenticated version of the document, indicating the governing software's approval, to be posted to the LLC's internal website. The governing software may from time to time update the terms of Appendix A under the following procedures . . . ."
- "If the LLC is served with a lawsuit, or if the governing software emits an authenticated document indicating that a lawsuit is to be filed by the

under RULLCA, step two in the list in the text is not constrained temporally to occur in the order in which it is listed; it may occur before step one.

LLC, a lawyer will be selected by the governing software and hired according to the following terms . . . ."

This can go on for pages if necessary. The goal is just to avoid any ambiguity about what the governing software can do. Specific clauses like this add very little (legally or logically) to a general clause that enables the governing software, but theoretically they serve only to decrease risk, and risk-averse lawyers are used to drafting agreements that appear needlessly cumbersome just on the off-chance that a minor clause will be useful one day.

The other provision in the second step above calls for the LLC not to dissolve when the last member dissociates from (i.e., formally terminates their membership with) the LLC. This step is more controversial and is described in more detail later in this section.

The third step is just icing on the cake. A legal entity can own property, so it can own the physical and intellectual property associated with whatever apparatus the organizers of a planned autonomous LLC want to place in control over the LLC. This step is intended to make the resulting LLC more autonomous in the sense that it eliminates certain types of interference by outsiders: if the LLC owns all legal rights to the computer software and hardware that is operating the LLC, it removes the opportunity for third parties to make property claims against that software and hardware in a way that could compromise the independence of the LLC.

After these three steps, the LLC is already meaningfully controlled by software and is, in many respects, already autonomous. But it is formally bound to the individual human member's will because an individual member of an LLC, at least by default, can replace the operating agreement with a new one. (Chapter 4 discusses possible self-limitations on that ability as a way to increase the autonomy of even LLCs that have members, as opposed to zero-member LLCs.) To avoid this sort of ongoing influence by or dependence on an individual member, the member should dissociate. An organization isn't fully autonomous until it can operate on its own, without influence by the people who set it up.

To understand the resulting organization's perpetual autonomy after step four above, it is important to recognize that under many modern LLC acts, the sole member's dissociation from the LLC does not require that the LLC terminate its existence. Indeed, many acts specifically contemplate at least the temporary continuation of a memberless LLC because this is a convenient option in several practical cases, such as estate planning. For example, parents might set up an LLC to hold a family's assets and adopt an agreement that states that on the death of the last surviving parent, the couple's children have the option to join the LLC.[117] The modern Uniform Limited Liability Company Act – known as RULLCA – accommodates this possibility, specifically providing that an LLC may by default continue to exist for ninety days without any members.[118]

Thus, at the very least, RULLCA clearly permits the creation of a new entity governed only by agreement – and thus by algorithm or process[119] – for up to ninety days. This is not insignificant; it would, for example, be sufficient to enable an algorithm to enter "its own" short-term service contracts with third parties during the ninety-day period that the uniform statute permits by default. It could also allow an autonomous LLC to perpetuate itself in small steps by setting up a new LLC that lasts for ninety days, and so on.

But RULLCA's permission extends further. The apparent ninety-day limitation, perhaps surprisingly, is not a mandatory rule imposed by the uniform statute. RULLCA Section 105(c) lists the statute's mandatory, nonwaivable provisions. That list explicitly refers to other criteria that might cause dissolution of an LLC – specifically, to applications by members for court-ordered dissolution as a result of fraud, oppression, or general illegality – but does not include, as inviolate, the ninety-day window for zero-member LLCs. In the 2006 version of RULLCA, the official comment to the act's provision on LLC dissolution expressly identified two other causes of dissolution, noting that they were "non-waivable,"[120] and did not say the same thing about the

---

[117] The parents may desire this structure (compared to one in which the children are members) as a convenient way to avoid having any legal obligations within the company to their children during their lifetimes.

[118] RULLCA § 701(a)(3) ("A limited liability company is dissolved, and its activities must be wound up, upon . . . the passage of 90 consecutive days during which the company has no members.").

[119] *See supra* text accompanying notes 93–94.

[120] RULLCA § 701 cmt. (2006 version, without 2013 amendments).

"90 consecutive days during which the company has no members" provision.[121] In the 2013 amendments to RULLCA, the official comment to the section on dissolution became even more explicit: "Except for [the ability for members to petition courts to dissolve the LLC and for administrative dissolution by the state government], this section compromises [sic] default rules."[122]

As a result, under RULLCA it is remarkably straightforward to set up a perpetual LLC that has no members in its final, planned operational state; to achieve it, one just needs to realize that it is possible. RULLCA is a uniform act adopted by the Uniform Law Commission, which does not itself make the statute law in the various US jurisdictions, but according to the Uniform Law Commission's records, eighteen jurisdictions have enacted RULLCA so far, usually with small variations. These jurisdictions include Connecticut, DC, Florida, Illinois, New Jersey, Pennsylvania, and Vermont. Importantly, people from out of state can usually make use of a state's LLC laws, and as I will describe in more detail in Chapter 4, only one of these states would need to approve of my technique for it to be usable throughout the country.

Moreover, RULLCA is not unique in recognizing memberless entities, and some states' particular statutes come very close to making explicit the possibility of perpetual memberless entities. For example, New York's LLC statute provides that an LLC "shall" terminate if

> at any time there are no members, provided that, unless otherwise provided in the operating agreement, the limited liability company is not dissolved and is not required to be wound up if, within one hundred eighty days *or such other period as is provided for in the operating agreement after the occurrence of the event that terminated the continued membership of the last remaining member,* the legal representative of the last remaining member agrees in writing to continue the limited liability company and to the admission of the legal representative of such member or its assignee to the limited liability company as a member, effective as of the occurrence of the event that terminated the continued membership of the last remaining member . . . .[123]

---

[121] *Id.*
[122] RULLCA § 701 cmt. (2006 version, 2013 amendments).
[123] N.Y. LTD. LIAB. CO. L. § 701(a)(1)(4) (emphasis added).

While the statute does contemplate that a memberless LLC will eventually have a new member, it explicitly gives the drafter of the operating agreement discretion as to the period during which the entity needn't have members. The statute permits, for example, the operating agreement to provide for a million-year period during which the LLC needn't have members. Again, during that period, the entity is governed only by agreement, not by the votes of members. It would be uncontroversial for the agreement to dictate, for example, a simple algorithm by which small payments were made.[124] Under the techniques of Chapter 2, however, the agreement can effectively delegate all decision-making powers to autonomous software.[125]

---

[124] On a larger scale, the LLC may have employees who continue operating the LLC without any members. The employees' powers would be determined ultimately by the operating agreement. It would not be unusual, for example, for a financially significant LLC in New York with a few employees to continue operating the entity normally while the operating agreement's process for determining new members proceeded separately, unaffected by (and not directly affecting) any operational concerns. If this situation arose in the context of a "family LLC" used by a wealthy family for the purposes of estate planning, I suspect the basic operation of the LLC, during its memberless period, would be uncontroversial except for substantive ambiguities in the operating agreement.

[125] Moreover, as I have previously put it, "The permission of just a single state would be sufficient to enable autonomous businesses. An organizer of such a business merely would need to select the organizational law of a state that permits a perpetual autonomous LLC." Bayern, *supra* note 83, at 1497. I elaborate on this notion in Chapter 4. As I discuss more fully there, to act in other states a business would ordinarily need to register as a foreign LLC, but (1) this step is often neglected with minimal results apart from limiting the ability of the entity to file a lawsuit in state court until the LLC corrects the technical registration defect, and (2) in any event, registration of a foreign LLC does not ordinarily alter its internal affairs, such as membership status or rights. This is a result of the general internal-affairs doctrine, a conflict-of-law rule that causes courts to defer on organizational matters to an entity's state of organizations. *See* Edgar v. Mite Corp., 457 U.S. 624, 645 (1982) ("The internal affairs doctrine is a conflict of laws principle which recognizes that only one State should have the authority to regulate a corporation's internal affairs.").

A further note: Even under an LLC act that does not permit memberless entities, the theoretical – and certainly the practical – possibility of *entity cross-ownership* enables very similar possibilities. The proposed technique is as follows: (1) Existing person *P* establishes member-managed LLCs *A* and *B*, with identical operating agreements each providing that the entity is controlled by an autonomous system that is not a preexisting legal person; (2) *P* causes *A* to be admitted as a member of *B* and *B* to be admitted as a member of *A*; (3) *P* withdraws from both entities. The result does not trigger the law's response to memberless entities, because what remains are simply two entities with one member each. Corporate statutes often have formal provisions that prevent this sort of cross-ownership from functioning successfully in corporations – at least as concerns the voting rights of shares – but there do not appear to be similar restrictions on LLCs, which of course in general provide for greater flexibility in

The end result is novel legal personhood – or at least a functional analogue or likeness of it – without any ongoing commitment by or subservience to a preexisting person. The range of legal action for this novel legal person is simply anything that the underlying entity can engage in. Under modern business-entity statutes, that range is exceedingly broad. For example, under RULLCA, "A limited liability company may have any lawful purpose, regardless of whether for profit."[126]

Of course, for a system to work with comprehensive functional autonomy today, it would probably need to be smart enough to know how to hire a lawyer if the entity is sued, or else it could be subject to arbitrary default judgments.[127] But the capacity for such hiring could be programmed formulaically (or, for example, a lawyer could be hired on retainer from the start of the entity's existence with the power only to respond defensively to lawsuits) without significant advances in artificial intelligence and, depending on the way the operating agreement is written, without significantly limiting the autonomy of the organization.

If legislatures do not like this possibility, they can easily amend the LLC acts to prevent the particular path toward autonomous organizations that I have described here. As I discuss in the next chapter, however, (1) it would be very difficult, in practice and as a systemwide matter, to achieve the goal of preventing autonomous organizations by means of statutory intervention, and (2) there is no indication, outside the more pessimistic varieties of science fiction, that states or other jurisdictions have any desire to do so. As of this writing, Congress has recently passed a statute that aims to reduce money laundering and other financial frauds by requiring that entities report their "beneficial owners," and in principle, at least within the United

arrangements of control and organization. *Cf., e.g.,* MBCA § 7.21(b) ("Shares of a corporation are not entitled to vote if they are owned by or otherwise belong to the corporation directly, or indirectly through an entity of which a majority of the voting power is held directly or indirectly by the corporation or which is otherwise controlled by the corporation."). See Chapter 4 for more discussion of this idea.

[126] RULLCA § 108(b). In considering autonomous organizations, the other subsections of Section 108 may be helpful to keep in mind as well: Section 108(a) reads "A limited liability company is an entity distinct from its member or members"; Section 108(c) reads "A limited liability company has perpetual duration."

[127] *See, e.g.,* FED. R. CIV. P. 55.

States, federal legislation could go a long way toward curtailing autonomous organizations.[128] However, the recent federal legislation does not curtail them, and even if it did, Chapter 2's techniques would still stand, and Chapter 4 provides a blueprint for various workarounds.[129]

Accordingly, my technique suggests a useful potential regulatory model for legal personhood. Under this model, legal personhood is like fire: its capabilities can be granted by anyone who already has it. Though it depends on the operation of public statutes, it functions largely as a peer-to-peer process, rather than a top-down bestowal from the government directly or a centralized process based on authoritatively recognized characteristics of the software in question. It avoids potentially intractable puzzles about precisely when, or upon attaining which characteristics, a system or process should have legal personhood – or at least it devolves those questions to anyone who already has that status. It is not a grant of legal personhood itself, but it is the next best thing: the ability to gain full control over a legal person, at least as a matter of the internal governance of that legal person.

3.4 MODELS OF PRIVATE-LAW PERSONHOOD FOR SOFTWARE

The previous section described the book's foundational technique for enabling an autonomous system, with the help of an existing legal person, to establish a functional analogue of novel personhood in its own right. The result is not literal legal personhood but, as just suggested, the opportunity to control a legal person without potential interference from the preexisting legal entities that established it. It is worth emphasizing that the techniques I have described do not provide a new source of *formal* legal personhood; they simply enable existing legal entities to confer a *functional* version of entity status (that is, the opportunity to control a new entity) on arbitrary systems, processes, or algorithms of their choosing. Of course, once one autonomous organization exists, it can use its functional powers as

---

[128] *See infra* notes 180–83 and accompanying text.
[129] *See id.* Note also that the policy in legislatures at the moment appears to be to encourage, rather than to discourage, software-based entities. *See, e.g., supra* notes 12 and 20.

the operator of an entity to create other entities; the "individual member" in my description above could well be a zero-member LLC itself.[130]

To begin to analyze the capabilities and motivations for software personhood, it will be helpful to consider the role of legal personhood generally in a modern system of private law.

3.4.1 Frameworks for Granting Legal Personhood

There are at least three ways in which a legal system might manage questions about the legal personhood of novel systems, such as software systems of varying degrees of autonomy and intelligence. First, it might be restricted to predefined groups of natural systems, like all humans or a subset of humans. I call this the *denialist* model, and in its pure form, it is too extreme for essentially all modern, mature legal systems, which bestow legal personhood on organizations as a way to provide a convenient interface between organizations and the rest of the private law. The recognition of organizations as legal persons – again, for the purposes of private law, not for the purposes of political questions like participation in the electoral system, free-speech rights, and so on – is so deeply embedded in our system that it would be impractical to root it out now. Nobody objects to receiving a check from a corporation; in fact, it is odder in most people's views to receive, as they do in many states, a local tax bill from an individual appointed as the local tax collector rather than from an organizational body, like a municipality.[131] But a softer version of the denialist model might recognize existing legal persons while refusing to extend the concept to novel systems.

Second, legal personhood might be bestowed only by public bodies – legislatures or administrative agencies – upon reasoned

---

[130] It is uncontroversial and commonplace for legal organizations to create new legal organizations. For example, an LLC or a corporation can create a new LLC (if, for example, it desires to spin off a division as an independent subsidiary). Nothing in the process formally requires a natural person. *Cf. infra* note 183.

[131] Similarly, lawyers and law students often puzzle over the arcane – and ultimately pointlessly formalistic – distinctions that underlie why "the United States" is a party to some legal proceedings whereas individually named or titled government officials are parties to others. The same arcane and pointless details apply to contracts entered into by officials of the federal government.

determinations of the capabilities or other attributes of a candidate person, such as a robot, a nonhuman animal, or a software system. I call this the *regulatory* model of legal personhood.

Most conventional analyses of legal personhood appear to assume that the law must choose between one or another of these models – that is, that the law must either adopt a policy of denying the expansion of legal personhood or must evaluate the capabilities of a new candidate system before making specific decisions about the legal personhood to which it should be entitled.[132] But there is a third model based on the transactional techniques described here: legal personhood, in its minimal private-law sense, can be treated as a status that can be bestowed, at least in function, by anyone who already possesses it. I call this the *grantable* model.

Current law already provides a hybrid, grantable notion of legal personhood: legal personhood may of course be granted by legislation, but the legislation associated with organizational law (RUPA, corporate law, and LLC acts) permits it to be granted by private parties subject to regulated procedures. The organizational-law model provides a potentially powerful conceptual insight: everything works fine when legal entities proliferate. Creating millions of legal entities doesn't create unmanageable complication; entity law simply acts as a conduit between other areas of law, like contract law or agency law. At the

---

[132] *See, e.g.*, Susan W. Brenner, *Humans and Humans+: Technological Enhancement and Criminal Responsibility*, 19 B.U. J. Sci. & Tech. L. 215, 285 (2013) ("I suspect [the law's concern with "how to enforce basic fairness and morality between a mix of human beings with varying abilities and also, perhaps, intelligent robots, cyborgs, chimeras, animals and alien beings"] will have to change even more if and when law decides to admit 'objects' (e.g., robots), animals (enhanced or not), semi-humans (cyborgs and chimeras) or space aliens to the 'legal person' club currently monopolized by Standard human beings."); Jack M. Beard, *Autonomous Weapons and Human Responsibilities*, 45 Geo. J. Int'l. L. 617, 663 (2014) (at least given current levels of technology, "[h]olding a robot accountable as a 'legal' person for war crimes as if it were a human appears to be impractical on many levels"); Bert-Jaap Koops et al., *Bridging the Accountability Gap: Rights for New Entities in the Information Society?*, 11 Minn. J.L. Sci. & Tech. 497, 511 (2010) ("Depending on how novel legal persons are introduced, they could, in fact, destabilize familiar notions of responsibility that form the moral core of the law, reinforcing undesirable affordances of an increasingly independent technological infrastructure."); Lawrence B. Solum, *Legal Personhood For Artificial Intelligences*, 70 N.C. L. Rev. 1231, 1243 (1992) ("How then should the law answer the question whether an AI can become a legal person and serve as a trustee? The first inquiry, I should think, would be whether the AI is competent to administer the trust.").

boundaries, maybe a proliferation of entities helps enable certain types of fraud, tax shelters, and the like, but that has led to very little pressure to stop the proliferation of organizations themselves.

It is worth adding that there are other potential models of legal personhood that may also be useful to consider briefly. For example, suppose that a state court were to hold that its jurisdiction LLC statute prohibits the technique that I have described in this chapter. In this case, it may still be difficult to determine who might bring an action to declare that the entity is dissolved. If only a public official (for example, the manager of the state department that regulates business entities) has that capability, then legal personhood becomes something that anyone can grant but only a particular, authorized public official can remove. Similarly, if any private party that interacts with a memberless LLC can sue to have it dissolved, legal personhood becomes something that anyone can grant but that requires the passive acknowledgement of certain other private parties.

3.4.2 Formal versus Substantive Legal Personhood

As another way to put it, formal legal personhood is simply, as it turns out, not that important. Allowing it to proliferate is not a significant practical change to the law. This is true for several reasons.

First, regardless of the application of personhood to autonomous organizations, private parties can already create legal entities for arbitrary purposes. They can even do so without formally registering them with the state, because it seems the state has little reason to keep track of legal entities. The most common mechanism by which parties can create an unregistered entity involves the "accidental" creation of for-profit general partnerships, a process that is well-understood (though contentious in the details) under historical partnership law and under RUPA.[133] For organizations that don't have a business purpose, unregistered unincorporated not-for-profit associations can be generated in lightweight fashion, privately and without registration with the state, and these are legal persons

---

[133] *See* RUPA § 202(a) ("[T]he association of two or more persons to carry on as co-owners a business for profit forms a partnership, whether or not the persons intend to form a partnership."); *see also* Bayern, *supra* note 113 (discussing the "accidental" formation of partnerships).

too.[134] A newer, less explored mechanism for creating a range of entities without separate state registration is to take advantage of state acts, such as Delaware's, that provide for *series LLCs*.[135] For technical readers familiar with operating-system theory and practice, a series LLC is to an LLC as a thread is to a process; a less technical metaphor, perhaps, is that a series LLC is like a web-browser tab whereas an LLC is like a web-browser window. Series LLCs permit the creation of large numbers of LLCs under the auspices of a single registered LLC; unlike the main LLC, the subordinate LLCs do not individually need to be registered with the state. Though the concept of series LLCs has raised conceptual problems for lawyers and lawmakers, the problems are detail-oriented and don't threaten to destabilize the whole legal system any more than the informal creation of thousands of general partnerships as legal entities does.

Second, legal personhood – again, in the minimal private-law sense in which I use the term – simply does not confer radical capabilities. Any autonomous system that desires (if it is sufficiently advanced to experience desire) – or for which others desire – legal personhood can approximate its capabilities with any willing human collaborator (or indeed any existing legal person that is willing). For example, an

---

[134] *See* Unif. Unincorporated Nonprofit Assoc. Act § 5(a) (2008) (last amended 2011) [hereinafter UUNAA] ("An unincorporated nonprofit association is an entity distinct from its members and managers."); *id.* § 2(11) ("'Unincorporated nonprofit association' means an unincorporated organization consisting of [two] or more members joined under an agreement that is oral, in a record, or implied from conduct, for one or more common, nonprofit purposes."); *id.* § 2 cmt. (noting that "the agreement to form a nonprofit association can be quite informal and sketchy" and adding that the word "agreement" in the definition was used "rather than 'contract' ... because the legal requirements for an agreement are less stringent and less formal than for a contract"). UUNAA, which like RUPA and RULLCA is a uniform act promulgated by the Uniform Law Commission, has been adopted by six US jurisdictions so far, according to the Commission.

[135] *See* Del. Ltd. Liab. Co. Act § 18-215(a) ("A limited liability company agreement may establish or provide for the establishment of 1 or more designated series of members, managers, limited liability company interests or assets. Any such series may have separate rights, powers or duties with respect to specified property or obligations of the limited liability company ... and any such series may have a separate business purpose or investment objective.").

Indeed, the essence of series LLCs may well be the ability to create a multitude of legal entities without direct, ongoing interaction with the government. Under general partnership law, even though conceptually the same partners might create many accidental "series partnerships," courts do not seem to have recognized that possibility. Nothing in RUPA prevents it, but because general partnerships do not confer limited liability, there seems to be little reason for partners to argue that they have created a multitude of distinct, transaction-specific general partnerships.

intelligent robot that wishes to own real property (or, more mundanely, a conventional computer program whose developer wishes for it to trade on their financial account) can achieve ends very similar to those that legal personhood provides without legal personhood, so long as there is a single enabler among the eight billion humans on the planet.

For example, suppose I develop a software system and open a bank account for the system in my name, and suppose that using that account, the system is able to earn some money from third parties. As a legal person, I simply can use the "system's" funds to purchase a house for the system's use, functioning as its practical, substantive, and economic (though not legal) agent. This works much as, in a darker legal time, husbands acted legally for their wives. For anything due respect, is not a praiseworthy arrangement; it invites control and dependence. But it helps demonstrate that autonomous organizations are not likely to be dangerous: if they were, they would need just one human being to open the door to the dangers, and we almost certainly would have seen the resulting problems by now.

As with a trust, no new legal person needs to be created in order to permit one person to act to achieve impersonal goals.[136] Consequently, legal personhood begins to look mostly like a bookkeeping mechanism – or like a way of simplifying the law's terminology and accounting – rather than a substantive grant of rights. Surely a sophisticated robot (or, again, the sophisticated developer of a conventional program or machine that acts in some sense autonomously) could arrange for a conventional entity, like a corporation, to be created; it would be very difficult for any party to interfere unilaterally with the entity creator's original plan for the entity, which plan could include arbitrary purposes such as the functional empowerment of an autonomous system. An autonomous organization does not create new substantive or economic powers; it just clarifies what is happening.

Third, even without the techniques described earlier in this chapter, enforcement of the technicalities internal to organizational entities is rare and difficult, at least where violations of those technicalities don't directly

---

[136] As observed *supra* note 7, trusts have long been permitted to aid impersonal beneficiaries, as in a "pet trust" that provides for the care of an animal. For the modern version of these, *see, e.g.*, www.aspca.org/pet-care/pet-planning/pet-trust-primer [https://perma.cc/EBL7-82EA].

harm anyone's substantive interests. The registration of organizations is notoriously messy and inaccurate; state corporation and LLC records are often not updated, for example, when membership changes, or perhaps even when an organization terminates.[137] In practice, if an LLC files a statement of authority naming a particular human agent – something I suspect would be commonplace for an LLC controlled by at least some types of autonomous systems – most banks, trading partners, and so on will be able to rely on the agent's authority without worrying about the LLC's peculiar structure, just as they already may do when dealing with conventional LLCs. Even if a memberless LLC were an illegal structure for an LLC to adopt, who would ever object in most cases?

Indeed, if it were unconcerned about observing all legal niceties, a sufficiently capable autonomous system, years in the future, could probably get away with simply visiting a state's website and organizing an LLC using the name and address of a willing human surrogate or patsy who would need no ongoing practical involvement with the entity. Or, indeed, our rogue intelligence may use an entirely made-up name and address, because states do not routinely authenticate information when filing requests for organizational registration. At least for mundane transactions, the operation of such an entity would probably not trigger any practical public scrutiny, and no private parties would have reason (or perhaps standing) to object. The result is simply a kind of impersonation of a legitimate legal person – a sort of legal analogue to a successful performance on the Turing Test. Chapter 4 discusses this line of thinking in more detail, and Chapters 5 and 6 explore the costs and benefits of this chapter's implications.

3.5 CONCLUSION

Though autonomous systems cannot participate in today's legal system as legal persons, this chapter offers a legal technique by which they might achieve something similar: the possibility of inhabiting a business organization (a legal person) of a type that is so flexible that the system's

---

[137] Federal efforts currently underway may clean up some of the messiness. *See infra* notes 180–83 and accompanying text.

operation can drive the entity's legal decisions. This possibility is not as radical as it sounds; it is available today so long as the autonomous system has at least one willing collaborator from the set of preexisting legal persons. The flexibility of modern LLCs makes such collaboration technically unnecessary, leading to a surprising possibility: effective legal personhood for nonhuman systems without wide-ranging legal reform and without resolving, as a precondition, any philosophical questions concerning the mind, personhood, or capabilities of nonhuman systems.

To be sure, "effective" legal personhood is not the same thing as real legal personhood. Even if their creators use my technique, autonomous systems have neither legal "equality" with humans nor any direct, de jure legal personhood. They can simply operate or maneuver a legal person to achieve arbitrary legal ends. In functional terms, however, this is probably a distinction without a difference; it is like saying that a human being's nervous system is not itself a legal person and that it can function only by "driving" a system – a whole human being – recognized by the law.

Still, de facto private-law personhood is different from full legal recognition in several ways. For one thing, the private law is not the totality of the law, and the techniques I have described say nothing about, for example, the criminal regulation of autonomous systems; this leads to some of the potential problems and implications for the law discussed in Chapter 6. For another, the mapping of an autonomous system to a memberless entity needn't be one-to-one; the same software system may operate multiple entities, for example – much as a single human can operate multiple LLCs, as distinct from how someone with multiple personalities *cannot*, using the concepts of basic legal personhood alone, act as multiple legal people.[138] The point is simply that just as business entities provide a legal alter ego for natural persons, they can conceptually provide a legal alter ego for things that are not natural persons. Just as conventional corporations can operate by process, algorithm, or agreement without direct human oversight in all cases, so might a new type of entity operate in such a manner indefinitely. Though a nonhuman autonomous system is merely the

---

[138] Similar techniques to those described in this chapter could be used, in principle, to "isolate" a single human being's multiple personalities from one another by means of carefully structured LLC operating agreements, at least in theory and under certain factual conditions.

"instrumentality" of a legal person under existing law, modern LLC law gives the autonomous system the opportunity to identify so closely with a novel type of legal person that it effectively becomes its own instrumentality. This is a meaningful type of capability even if the system never formally acquires legal personhood.

Importantly, these possibilities are not just conceptual. The techniques I have described work under existing law. The next chapter explores the positive legal viability of these techniques in more detail.

4 THE LEGAL VIABILITY OF AUTONOMOUS ORGANIZATIONS

One reaction to the techniques discussed in the Chapter 3 has been honest horror: "The survival of the human race may depend" on rejecting the premises of my argument.[139] Others believe that perhaps I've identified a set of significant legal loopholes but that courts will shut them down or legislatures will close them. The main point of this chapter is that legal policymakers, like courts and legislatures, both (1) have little motivation to stop my techniques from being applied and (2) likely couldn't even if they wanted to, although anything is possible through strong federal legislation or constitutional amendments. A narrower point is that my reading of the current LLC statutes is the proper reading.

It is somewhat artificial, when discussing common law, to separate existing doctrine from the overall benefits, costs, and implications of the doctrine. The reason for this is that common law is grounded ultimately in morality and policy, and every case is an opportunity to change the law,[140] particularly when the cases concern novel transactional techniques and the far-reaching implications of new technologies.[141] That said, this chapter attempts to isolate and respond to the doctrinal objections to autonomous organizations under existing LLC statutes, whereas Chapters 5 and 6 discuss the overall benefits, costs, and implications of autonomous organizations. In short, this chapter defends what I've said so far in this book as the correct view of LLC statutes and the modern framework of organizational law – a proposition that has been challenged

---

[139] LoPucki, *supra* note 24, at 953.
[140] *See* MELVIN A. EISENBERG, THE NATURE OF THE COMMON LAW 14–19 (1988).
[141] *See* Shawn Bayern, *Against Certainty*, 41 HOFSTRA L. REV. 53 (2012).

by people who have been resistant to the idea of autonomous organizations.

For example, in a series of online essays and eventually an article in the *Nevada Law Journal*, Matt Scherer has attempted to show that my transactional techniques won't work under current LLC statutes.[142] The main force of his criticism, though he doesn't put it in quite these words, is that what I propose is too crazy for courts to tolerate. Maybe, his argument runs, it's an acceptable literal reading of various LLC statutes, but autonomous entities would clearly violate the statutes' intent and structure, and courts would stop them the way they'd stop other sorts of technical abuses of statutes and regulations.[143]

That type of criticism is mistaken, and simply as a matter of positive law my reading of the LLC statutes is correct. To be clear, my blueprint for creating autonomous LLCs is just a product of current statutes; with appropriate legislative will, particularly at the federal level, they could all be repealed or curtailed in due course, and my goal here is not to discuss other, nonstatutory sources of legal capabilities for algorithms, although I have touched on others in passing throughout this book.[144] My goal in this chapter is simply to show that the statutes do

---

[142] Scherer, *supra* note 29, Matthew Scherer, *Is AI Personhood Already Possible Under U.S. LLC Laws? (Part One: New York)*, www.lawandai.com/2017/05/14/is-ai-personhood-already-possible-under-current-u-s-laws-dont-count-on-it-part-one/ [https://perma.cc/B2TK-DFCV] [hereinafter Scherer, *Part One*]; Matthew Scherer, *Is AI Personhood Already Possible Under U.S. LLC Laws? (Part Two: Uniform LLC Act)*, www.lawandai.com/2017/05/21/is-ai-personhood-already-possible-under-current-u-s-laws-part-two-uniform-llc-act/ [https://perma.cc/K7BS-27Y5]; Matthew Scherer, *Is AI Personhood Already Possible Under U.S. LLC Laws? (Part Three)*, www.lawandai.com/2017/06/18/is-ai-personhood-already-possible-under-u-s-llc-laws-part-three/ [https://perma.cc/R6K6-6X8Q].

[143] *Cf.* 26 U.S.C. § 7701(o)(5)(a) ("The term 'economic substance doctrine' means the common law doctrine under which tax benefits … with respect to a transaction are not allowable if the transaction does not have economic substance or lacks a business purpose."); *id.* § 7701(o)(1) ("In the case of any transaction to which the economic substance doctrine is relevant, such transaction shall be treated as having economic substance only if (A) the transaction changes in a meaningful way (apart from Federal income tax effects) the taxpayer's economic position, and (B) the taxpayer has a substantial purpose (apart from Federal income tax effects) for entering into such transaction.") (paragraph spacing adjusted).

[144] For example, to the extent that agreements can recognize algorithms as discussed in Chapter 2, there are many other potential interfaces between algorithms and existing law apart from LLC statutes. Most simply, an algorithm may direct some of the activities of an existing, conventional legal entity even if it does not control the entirety of that entity – precisely to the extent that a conventional contract may do so, which is to say the capability is quite broad but still subordinate to the LLC's operating agreement. Other

what I say they do and that it would be both odd and exceedingly difficult for courts to stop the statutes from working in the way I describe. That may seem like a relatively narrow point, but it is important: if even a single state's court interprets LLC statutes as I suggest, then autonomous organizations can be created in that state and would almost certainly, under current law, be recognized elsewhere. (Moreover, it would be very hard to stop them from working elsewhere.)

This chapter proceeds in several stages. First, I describe how, as a practical matter, nothing is likely to stop variants of my technique from working if private actors intend for them to work.[145] In other words, my technique is viable de facto, regardless of technical statutory interpretation or legal theory. Then, I give a more thorough legal justification for my interpretive view of the LLC statutes, defending it de jure rather than just practically.

As a reminder, the result of Chapter 3's techniques is an LLC with no members, governed by an operating agreement that gives legal effect to the decisions of an autonomous system. No other legal person remains behind to govern the LLC internally. Of course, the LLC is still subject both to external regulation and to LLC law; for example, like any LLC, it might face regulatory prohibitions, and the state or other eligible parties might bring an action against it for administrative dissolution. But the autonomous system has gained a significant amount of freedom: it can act legally for an entity without the internal governance of that entity being in the hands of any separate legal person.

4.1 THE FOCUS OF THE OBJECTIONS TO AUTONOMOUS ORGANIZATIONS

For convenience, the four steps in my transactional approach, spelled out in more detail in the previous chapter, are as follows:

---

potential existing legal sources for the capabilities of algorithms apart from contract law include trust law and the common law of unincorporated associations.

[145] Matt Scherer appears to accept this argument. *See* Scherer, *Part One*, *supra* note 142 ("I do not see any provisions that would obviously prevent or even discourage such a setup.").

(1) As a single member, create a member-managed LLC.
(2) Cause the LLC to adopt an operating agreement that (a) defers operating decisions of the LLC to an algorithm and (b) provides that the LLC will continue to exist even after the last member dissociates.
(3) Transfer ownership of any relevant physical and intellectual property to the LLC.
(4) Withdraw from the LLC, leaving the LLC without any members.

In the outline above, step one is clearly uncontroversial; everyone today believes that a single-member LLC is possible, although it is worth noting that even a single-member company was once regarded as a controversial type of entity, arising out of what was considered a loophole a few generations ago.[146] (Its commonplace occurrence today suggests the flexibility of business-entity law, a point to which I will return later in this chapter.)

Step two is largely unchallenged, and I defended this step more thoroughly in Chapters 2 and 3. In short, one possible objection to step two, suggested (although not specifically applied to this transactional technique) by the work of my colleague Lauren Scholz, is that an operating agreement that defers in an open-ended manner to the operation of software may be too indefinite to be enforced.[147] But as discussed in Chapter 2, modern contract law appears uncontroversially to enforce agreements far more indefinite than the ones that step two requires, and in any event the LLC's operating agreement can be made as definite as necessary.

---

[146] *See* Bernard F. Cataldo, *Limited Liability with One-Man Companies and Subsidiary Corporations*, 18 LAW & CONTEMP. PROBS. 473 (1953) ("It is most doubtful whether the concept of corporate enterprise was ever intended or designed to embrace this institution. Nevertheless the one-man company and the family corporation have become familiar modes of business enterprise and, despite occasional questioning by a court or a writer, have generally received judicial sanction and approval."); Warner Fuller, *The Incorporated Individual: A Study of the One-Man Company*, 51 HARV. L. REV. 1373, 1374 (1938) ("One accustomed to accept language at its face value would be at a loss to find authority for the creation or existence of [a one-person] corporation in enabling legislation. With rare exception the one-man corporation has not been expressly authorized under the general incorporation statutes, and if the language of the statutes is to be given its fair import, none would seem even to be contemplated.").

[147] *See generally* Scholz, *supra* note 25 (arguing that contracts that defer to algorithms may be too indefinite to be enforced).

Step three is uncontroversial because LLCs can clearly own tangible and intangible property.[148]

The main descriptive objection to the technique overall has been to step four. For example, Matt Scherer's objection is that courts simply would not allow an LLC to continue once the only member has dissociated or withdrawn.[149]

4.2 THE WORKABILITY OF LLCS WITHOUT ONGOING HUMAN INTERNAL GOVERNANCE

Most of the doctrinal critiques of my transactional techniques have tried to raise concerns about the law's acceptance of zero-member entities. As I will demonstrate later in this chapter, I don't think these critiques are correct. It is possible, however, to sidestep them entirely – that is, to achieve very similar results with transactional structures that appear less radical.

In other words, it may sound almost disappointing, but for purely practical purposes the technique that I introduced and developed in Chapter 3 is probably not *necessary* if the goal is to give software the ability to control an organization. Autonomous organizations are possible – for practical purposes – without even raising questions about whether modern law can and will support zero-member organizations.

As an example, two different but conceptually similar transactional techniques easily make it possible, as a purely practical matter, for a modern LLC to be governed in an ongoing fashion by an operating agreement (and hence an algorithm with verifiable state)[150] without regard to ongoing consent by the LLC's members. If the existing members' ability to govern an entity in ongoing fashion is limited, then those members will have little or no opportunity to interfere with the practical governance of the organizations. As a result, the software that the operating agreement empowers will have free rein, at least as an operational, pragmatic matter.

---

[148] *See* RULLCA § 1 cmt.
[149] *See* sources cited *supra* note 142.
[150] *See supra* note 33.

First, if membership is formally necessary for an LLC to exist under a particular LLC statute – that is, if there is a legal difference between having members and not having members – then groups of LLCs can be created that own one another, thereby using membership as the formal placeholder that it is but preserving the functional autonomy of the software that's really in charge of the LLC. Second, operating agreements may establish a default state of affairs and make it practically impossible, because of procedural requirements and other "veto gates," for any preexisting legal persons or collections of them to adjust this default state. Both of these techniques empower, in practice, an LLC's operating agreement or any verifiable system that the operating agreement recognizes. These techniques are both relatively uncontroversial and extraordinarily difficult for courts to police. Moreover, if even one state permits them, other states are unlikely to interfere with their operation on the ground that internal governance is a matter of the law of the state in which an entity is organized.[151]

The rest of this section discusses these two techniques in turn.

4.2.1 Cross-Ownership

The first of these techniques is achieved as follows:

(1) An individual member (the "Founder") creates two member-managed LLCs, A and B, filing the appropriate paperwork with the state. The LLCs each start with a single member, the Founder.
(2) The Founder causes each entity to adopt a desired operating agreement that sets the parameters under which each entity operates (e.g., deferring control to an algorithm).
(3) The Founder causes A to admit B as a member and B to admit A as a member.
(4) The Founder dissociates from both A and B.

At the end of this procedure, two entities exist. Each functions just as described in Chapter 3, acting only under the control of the operating agreement, which (for example) may defer all decisions to an algorithm. Accordingly, there is no practical need to press the point that the final member may dissociate, leaving a memberless entity.

---

[151] *E.g.*, RULLCA § 106.

In the classical American corporation, shares held in this form of cross-ownership are prevented by statute from voting because they would otherwise serve as a formal technique to cement control of an existing board of directors.[152] This prohibition is absent from the typical LLC statute, which generally does not attempt to address the policy concerns associated with the takeover of public entities or the defenses to those takeovers by the existing directors. The "freedom of contract" that conventionally underlies LLCs[153] includes the freedom to set up this sort of cross-ownership of voting shares. In any event, neither LLC would need to vote as a member of the other LLC to achieve the scheme's functional goal; the point is in fact that neither member has any functional power.

Of course, the cross-ownership structure needn't be as simple as outlined above. It could involve dozens of entities, some of which own others in various percentages. I mention this just to suggest that it would be difficult to prevent this technique from working. LLC operating agreements are normally private – they are not a matter of public record – and anyone attempting to unravel the precise ownership structure of a particular business organization potentially has a lot of work to do.[154] A simple legal structure, like the classical corporation, may have a simple capitalization table; if every share is the same, as it was in traditional corporations, then a single real number is sufficient to describe the nature and extent of a shareholder's ownership of a corporation.[155] (Similarly, in what we might think of as a prototypical

---

[152] *E.g.*, DEL. GEN. CORP. L. § 160(c) (2019) ("Shares of its own capital stock belonging to the corporation shall neither be entitled to vote nor be counted for quorum purposes; this includes shares belonging to another corporation, if a majority of the shares entitled to vote in the election of directors of such other corporation is held, directly or indirectly, by the corporation.").

[153] *See, e.g.*, DEL. LTD. LIAB. CO. ACT § 18-1101 (2016) ("It is the policy of this chapter to give the maximum effect to the principle of freedom of contract and to the enforceability of limited liability company agreements.").

[154] Recent federal legislation attempts to improve this situation, but it remains to be seen how it will address the potential complexities of business ownership and how effectively it will be enforced. *See infra* note 182.

[155] Today, it is common to see different *classes* or *series* of shares, each with different rights (reflecting different types of ownership, voting power, and so on), so the modern corporation shares some of the potential complexity of the modern LLC. Moreover, as discussed in Section 3.2, under modern corporation statutes the organizers of small corporations have immense flexibility to restructure the corporation – for example, by eliminating the board of directors entirely. *See* MBCA § 7.32(a)(1) (a shareholder

general partnership, two or three real numbers are sufficient to describe a partner's status: the amount of their capital account, their share of profits, and their share of losses. Of course, in practice partnerships can be much more complicated.) In an LLC, however, there is no fixed limit on the complexity of the ownership arrangements; an LLC could be owned by a cycle or web of hundreds of other LLCs. In all cases, the LLC would have members, but nothing would guarantee that there is an existing legal person, in the steady state, "behind" the various LLCs – with either power or substantive economic ownership over the entities.

4.2.2 Vetogates

Still, cross-ownership wouldn't foil a legal system that did somehow require human members ultimately to lie behind legal entities. Later in the chapter, I will show why legal systems are unlikely to impose such a requirement and why it would be unlikely to work in any event, but for now, it may be useful to develop a different type of technique that gives software autonomous control over a legal organization even while humans remain formally involved enough to satisfy a formalistic desire that legal entities not be fully autonomous from internal human governance.

In 1992, McNollgast (itself an artificial entity of sorts)[156] used the term "veto gates" to describe opportunities for legislation to be stopped; the notion is now familiar that many actors, practically speaking, need to approve legislation before it can be enacted.[157] Similar veto gates – now more typically written as *vetogates*[158] – can also easily arise, accidentally or by design, in private operating agreements written for

---

agreement is effective even if it "eliminates the board of directors or restricts the discretion or powers of the board of directors"). The result is that corporations and LLCs can reflect a very similar type of complexity in practice, today, even if each starts from a different set of assumptions and default rules.

[156] The name refers to a group of three authors of a series of significant articles. *See* McNollgast, "McNollgast," https://mcnollgast.stanford.edu/research/mcnollgast-2/ [https://perma.cc/78HR-6GP3].

[157] Others, most notably William Eskridge, have analyzed the role of "vetogates" extensively in public law. *See, e.g.*, William N. Eskridge Jr., *Vetogates and American Public Law*, 31 J. L. Econ. Org 756 (2015).

[158] *See generally id.*

legal organizations. For example, it is commonplace to see cases in which a small organization requires a supermajority of its members to change the status quo.[159] It is also possible – and not at all rare – for LLC operating agreements to create situations in which the members "deadlock," leading to indefinite periods during which the entity is paralyzed because nobody can act for it effectively.[160] Deadlock is commonplace enough that many LLC statutes aim to address it by giving courts the power to break deadlock by dissolving an entity upon suit by a member,[161] although the granting of such orders is extremely rare because courts are concerned not to destroy potentially productive businesses or pick sides among equally blameless (or blameworthy) parties.[162] Moreover, when deadlock is granted, it is ordinarily judged in view of the policies of the operating agreement; as a New York appellate court put it, "the only basis for dissolution [for deadlock] can be if [the entity] cannot effectively operate under the operating agreement to meet and achieve the purpose for which it was created."[163]

Accordingly, it is not difficult for the author of an LLC's operating agreement to write it in such a way that the owners, members, or managers – even if they do exist – are powerless figureheads. The imagination of lawyers is the only limit on how comprehensively such agreements might prevent changes to the status quo. To put it differently, even if the technique I described in Chapter 3 is not possible, drafters of operating agreements can approach its result – the triumph of an existing operating agreement over ongoing governance by members – asymptotically. A supermajority voting requirement is a simple, commonplace first step toward that destination – most people are familiar with, or at least can easily imagine, a group of people who could never make meaningful decisions if 80 or 90 percent of the members had to approve – but more creative techniques are possible.

---

[159] *E.g.*, Fisk Ventures, LLC v. Segal, C.A. No. 3017-CC, 2008 WL 1961156 (Del. Ch. May 7, 2008).

[160] *See id.*

[161] *See, e.g.*, Matter of Arrow Inv. Advisors, LLC, 2009 Del Ch LEXIS 66 ("Given its extreme nature, judicial dissolution is a limited remedy that this court grants sparingly.").

[162] *See, e.g.*, Matter of 1545 Ocean Ave., LLC, 72 A.D.3d 121, 131 (N.Y. App. 2010) ("Dissolution is a drastic remedy.").

[163] *Id.* at 130.

Imagine, for example, the appointment of a thousand members to a new LLC. Each of these members – chosen largely at random, with little connection to the other members, wide geographical and social dispersion, and so on – is paid a nominal sum to agree to become a member and assured that the limited-liability status of the entity means that they incur no, or at most negligible, personal risks for accepting that status.[164] Then, imagine that the operating agreement requires that any new business decisions (whether ordinary or extraordinary),[165] or any amendments to the agreement itself, require 990 of these 1000 members to constitute a quorum and agree. It would probably be hard to get a hundred of these members into the same meeting, much less to get 990 of them to agree on anything. And to prevent even the possibility of agreement, twenty of them could be asked to agree in advance – for yet another nominal sum – to vote "no" on every matter presented in the LLC's management meetings. Classical organizational law (such as the law of corporations in the early and mid-1900s) prevented or at least inhibited private parties from structuring the internal governance of an entity in this manner, in particular closely scrutinizing private agreements on how to vote.[166] But the animating principle of modern organizational law, which reaches its fulfillment in the law of LLCs, is again "freedom of contract" in matters of internal governance; these sorts of voting agreements are expressly permitted by modern law, even in corporations.[167] They should be uncontroversial in LLCs.

Of course, such extreme governance techniques will not ordinarily be necessary. A small group of individuals all interested in giving an autonomous system legal personhood probably would be sufficient to achieve the same result. Four humans in favor of autonomous organizations could create an entity governed by algorithm, all remain

---

[164] If this structural legal guarantee is not enough, the organizer may pay for further private insurance for the members or simply compensate them more for accepting the risk.

[165] The law of unincorporated businesses often draws a distinction between matters in the "ordinary course" of business, typically governed by default by a majority vote, and other matters, which typically require by default a supermajority or unanimity. *See, e.g.*, RUPA § 301.

[166] *See, e.g.*, MELVIN ARON EISENBERG & JAMES D. COX, CORPORATIONS AND OTHER BUSINESS ORGANIZATIONS 464–65 (10th ed.) (discussing the history of restrictions on voting agreements in corporate law).

[167] *E.g.*, MBCA § 7.31.

members, and write an operating agreement that requires their unanimous consent to interfere with the algorithm, along with private contracts not to interfere or seek dissolution. They would all be members or human representatives of the organization as a formal matter for any regulations that might require human members or representatives, but they would have no actual power because of their private contracts (and possibly because of the difficulty of reaching consensus).

Importantly, however, adding vetogates is meaningfully different from a simpler structure in which a single founder remains attached to an LLC just to keep the LLC from being dissolved by a legal system that requires business to have owners. That sort of arrangement may be effective in giving an algorithm the potential to have legal consequences, but it is fragile because it depends on the founder's ongoing cooperation. It provides no new meaningful freedom to the legal organization or the autonomous system that it was meant to enable, and it permits the founder – or the founder's creditors or heirs, if the founder becomes insolvent or dies – to appropriate any of the LLC's gains selfishly. But vetogates, complicated amendment procedures, and simple supermajority requirements among even a small group of individuals all present meaningfully more practical freedom for the entity, and they all make it less likely that any individual will be able to act selfishly in order to appropriate the assets of the LLC.

In short, an operating agreement's power is not an all-or-nothing proposition; agreements can be made more or less powerful simply by restricting the practical ability of members to interfere with their operation. Apart from the rarely exercised statutory power to dissolve an LLC because of deadlock – which, additionally, an organizer may attempt to hedge against through private contracting, particularly if the potential suits for deadlock are foreseen when an entity is organized[168] – vetogates confer an indefinitely large amount of power

---

[168] Under RULLCA § 701(a)(4)(B), a shareholder may sue for an LLC's dissolution if "it is not reasonably practicable to carry on the company's activities and affairs in conformity with the certificate of organization and the operating agreement." This provision, which does not refer to deadlock specifically, should be relatively easy to keep at bay by a properly worded operating agreement. The provision itself is not waivable – the operating agreement cannot get rid of it entirely – but the operating agreement can state clearly that (1) the purpose of the organization is to enable the independent activities of software, (2) ongoing deadlocks among members are specifically contemplated and

on an operating agreement at the expense of the future members or managers.

In analyzing the possibility of vetogates, it is important to recognize that nothing in the mandatory structure of modern LLCs requires that members be the economic beneficiaries of the entity, that members have any significant power, and so on; the structure of an LLC is flexible enough not to require any such traditional patterns.[169] Moreover, modern statutes have tended to make quite explicit that LLC agreements control the conditions of their own amendment[170]

---

should not be the basis for a judicial order of dissolution, and (3) various sorts of specifically contemplated activities of the organization, as a nonexclusive list, count as acting "in conformity with the with the ... operating agreement."

Moreover, as the comment to RULLCA § 105 points out, the operating agreement "may determine the forum in which a claim for dissolution under Section 701(a)(4) is determined. For example, arbitration and forum selection clauses are commonplace in business relationships in general and in operating agreements in particular." It is something of a legal fiction that changing the forum in which a dispute is to be heard doesn't change the substantive rights that underlie the dispute, but clearly, as a practical matter, the parties to an operating agreement might choose an AI-friendly mandatory arbiter.

A final note: under some states' LLC statutes, this sort of deadlock provision is waivable outright, at least in theory. The same comment to RULLCA § 105 observes that a Delaware court held in 2013 that "the right to judicial dissolution is a default right which the parties may eschew by contract" under Delaware's LLC statute. Huatuco v. Satellite Healthcare, CV 8465-VCG, 2013 Del. Ch. LEXIS 298, at *1 (Del. Ch. Dec. 9, 2013). Similarly, Fla. Stat. § 605.0105 – Florida's analogue to RULLCA's Section 105 – provides that operating agreements may not "[v]ary the grounds for dissolution" but specifically adds: "A deadlock resolution mechanism does not vary the grounds for dissolution for the purposes of this paragraph." Fla. Stat. § 605.105(i). Nothing in the statute prevents the deadlock-resolution mechanism from being algorithmic or implemented by software.

[169] E.g., Fla. Stat. § 605.0401(4) ("A person may become a member without acquiring a transferable interest and without making or being obligated to make a contribution to the limited liability company."). As a demonstration of the statutory trend toward increased flexibility and unconventional LLCs, the principal authors of the Florida LLC statute have described this provision as follows:

> New to Florida law, § 605.0401(4) provides that a person may become a member without acquiring an economic interest, and without making or being obligated to make a contribution to the LLC. This is a departure from existing law, which defines a member as a person with an economic interest in the LLC. This significant change permits springing members, facilitates special purpose LLCs, and allows for participation in governance by members with no economic interest in the company.

Louis T. M. Conti & Gregory M. Marks, *Florida's New Revised LLC Act, Part I*, 87 Fl. Bar J. 52 (2013), www.floridabar.org/the-florida-bar-journal/floridas-new-revised-llc-act-part-i/ [https://perma.cc/E9L6-QPQT].

[170] RULLCA § 105(a)(4) ("[T]he operating agreement governs ... the means and conditions for amending the operating agreement.").

and that those conditions can be flexible and unconventional, for example implicating people or events external to the LLC. For example as Section 107 of RULLCA currently puts it:

> An operating agreement may specify that its amendment requires the approval of a person that is not a party to the agreement or the satisfaction of a condition. An amendment is ineffective if its adoption does not include the required approval or satisfy the specified condition.[171]

Similarly, as the official comment to RULLCA describes, "the operating agreement can control both the quantum of consent required ... and the means by which the consent is manifested,"[172] and it specifically contemplates giving "a non-member veto rights over amendments to the agreement."[173] RULLCA clearly is not hostile to the notion that an operating agreement may be extremely difficult to amend.

More fanciful restrictions are possible. RULLCA's official comment's example of a "means by which consent is manifested" is "prohibiting modifications except when consented to in writing,"[174] but in principle an operating agreement could require skywriting, embossing the amendment on a solid-gold brick, completing the amendment on the moon, or anything else that increases the expense or practical difficulties of amendment. Note that while RULLCA prevents LLC operating agreements from being "manifestly unreasonable" in other areas (like modifications to statutory fiduciary duties), it does not impose that requirement for evaluating the procedure by which amendments to the operating agreement are permitted.[175] Its position is largely neutral on the matter: it simply wants to enable parties to choose how their own agreements are to be amended, if at all.

A quick reminder at this stage, before I justify the legality of Chapter 3's specific technique, may be helpful: just as for Chapter 3's

---

[171] RULLCA § 107. Under RULLCA §§ 407(b)(4)(B) and 407(c)(3)(B), by default an amendment to the operating agreement requires the "affirmative vote or consent of all ... members."
[172] RULLCA § 105 cmt.
[173] RULLCA § 107 cmt.
[174] RULLCA § 105 cmt.
[175] *See generally* RULLCA § 105.

technique, for the propositions about cross-ownership and vetogates that I have made here to be correct and practically significant, only one state would need to endorse them. Other states will not, under current law, interfere in the internal governance of an entity. To the extent that autonomous, algorithmically controlled entities become popular over time, organizers could easily choose the jurisdictions most favorable to their chosen vetogates or cross-ownership strategies.[176]

4.2.3 Defiance

There is a further practical consideration that would permit the same result as Chapter 3's technique even if courts refused to honor it. LLC operating agreements are private documents, generally not available to nonparties or to courts or governments in the abstract.[177] To challenge either of the techniques described above, or indeed Chapter 3's central technique, a third party would have to discover that it was being used and then prove it to the court. In the unlikely event that uses of these techniques were discovered by a private third party, those behind the techniques would have the opportunity to refashion private agreements as they saw fit – to cure anticipated legal problems for the duration of a court case, or even simply to dishonestly represent the nature of the relevant entities' internal governance.[178] And in the case of cross-ownership, the two related entities may be formed in different states

---

[176] *Cf. generally* William Cary, *Federalism and Corporate Law: Reflections Upon Delaware*, 83 YALE L.J. 663 (1974) (initiating a long-running debate about how the motivations for the choice of Delaware law among corporate organizers should influence legal policy at the national level).

[177] For example, RULLCA does not require that operating agreements be filed with the state. In practice, usually a barebones "certificate" or "charter" is filed and made public; this might list the registered agent for service of process and the initial members or managers of the entity. Few operating agreements for closely held organizations are made public, except incidentally through such processes as litigation or grant applications.

[178] As a formal matter, an actor willing to be dishonest, in possession of purely private documents, and able to change the documents before disclosing them to others has an entirely open canvas until any particular document needs to be disclosed, at which point only the previously disclosed documents serve as constraints. *Cf.* SANJEEV ARORA & BOAZ BARAK, COMPUTATIONAL COMPLEXITY: A MODERN APPROACH 260–61 (2009) (describing "adversary arguments" in analyzing the complexity of algorithms, but a similar concept applies broadly to proof of legal wrongdoing).

or even countries, potentially complicating discovery and even jurisdiction.

There is also, of course, a simpler sort of possible defiance: an algorithm or its promoter may simply provide false information when registering an LLC. Obviously I don't endorse this sort of illegal conduct; I'm merely observing that it's possible. Because criminals have been able to abuse the openness of entity-registration procedures in ways that have nothing to do with autonomous organizations, public authorities have recently been seeking to prevent this type of fraud. Thus, for example, the UK (which has a much more centralized system for registering companies than the United States) has recently added ID-verification requirements for the directors of registered companies.[179] In the US's decentralized, state-by-state model, it would be difficult for one state to make any progress along similar lines; for example, California could adopt requirements similar to the recent reforms to Companies House's procedures in the UK, but that wouldn't prevent an artificial intelligence from submitting fraudulent organizational documents for an LLC in Wyoming. And, of course, a formal procedure for verification is not enough to prevent abuse; such procedures need to be enforced to be effective. Thus, the traditional state of affairs in the United States has been that an artificial intelligence's practical ability to register a new LLC illicitly would depend on the likelihood of successful enforcement in the most lax US state, even if each state had enforcement procedures to begin with.

That general state of affairs may be changing with new federal legislation that seeks to require all companies registered in the United States to declare their beneficial owners using governmental IDs like passports.[180] Even if this new legislation is a practical success in preventing general fraud and money laundering – which remains to be seen – it stops neither autonomous organizations nor

---

[179] *See* Michael Cross, *Law ID Checks on Directors in Companies House Reforms*, L. Soc. GAZETTE, Sept. 18, 2020, www.lawgazette.co.uk/law/id-checks-on-directors-in-companies-house-reforms/5105695.article [https://perma.cc/EQ22-8M5X].

[180] Corporate Transparency Act of 2019, H.R. 2513, 116th Cong. (2019–2020); National Defense Authorization Act for Fiscal Year 2021, H.R. 6395 (2020); *see also* Jeanne Whalen, *Congress Bans Anonymous Shell Companies After Long Campaign by Anti-Corruption Groups*, Dec. 11, 2020, www.washingtonpost.com/us-policy/2020/12/11/anonymous-shell-company-us-ban/ [https://perma.cc/UFV4-6FG7].

certain types of defiance potentially associated with them. For example, the act requires only the filing of information about "beneficial owners,"[181] and autonomous organizations will have no beneficial owners;[182] they may have such owners at the time they are formed, but presumably the organizer of an autonomous organization can fully disclose their involvement at that time and thereby comply with the act.[183] Moreover, under some state LLC statutes, the concept of membership is distinct from the concept of beneficial ownership (and, of course, from management),[184] and this complexity may raise confusion about what is to be disclosed and how the law will be enforced. Given the privacy and potential complexity

---

[181] Corporate Transparency Act of 2019, *supra* note 180, § 3(a)(1) (to be codified at 31 U.S.C. § 5333(a)(1)).

[182] The Corporate Transparency Act defines "beneficial owners" to include natural persons who "exercise[] substantial control over a corporation or limited liability company," "own[] 25 percent or more of the equity interests of a corporation or limited liability company," or "receive[] substantial economic benefits from the assets of a corporation or limited liability company." *Id.* (to be codified at 31 U.S.C. § 5333(d)(3)(A)). It excludes children, nominees, and people who are only creditors. It is therefore easy for even a conventional entity to lack any "beneficial owners" merely through financial interest; that is, there is no requirement that even a conventional entity will have a financial (versus controlling) interest to report under the new law. *Id.* (to be codified at 31 U.S.C. § 5333 (d)(3)(B)).

In any event, nothing in the new statute appears to require that an organization have any beneficial owners, and it excludes nonprofit entities as long as they make necessary filings under the Internal Revenue Code, "if required." *Id.* (to be codified at 31 U.S.C. § 5333(d)(4)(xiii)). Accordingly, it appears to be straightforward for an organizer of an autonomous organization to comply with the act by simply identifying themselves properly when taking the initial steps to set up the organization; that requirement should pose little problem for law-abiding organizers of autonomous organizations.

Moreover, the law applies only to corporations and LLCs; it excludes, for example, limited partnerships and other organizational forms, although it commissions a study about those other organizational forms. *Id.* § 4(b). Autonomous organizations are possible under many states' organizational statutes for forms other than LLCs, following techniques very similar to those described in Chapter 3. *See supra* note 108.

[183] The act assumes that those who organize state entities will be natural persons – or at least it is concerned only with that type of organizer. That is, it defines "applicant" as "any natural person who files an application to form a corporation or limited liability company under the laws of a State or Indian Tribe," Corporate Transparency Act of 2019, *supra* note 180, § 3(a)(1) (to be codified at 31 U.S.C. § 5333(d)(1)), and imposes its core registration-time requirement on each such "applicant." *Id.* (to be codified at 31 U.S.C. § 5333(a)(1)(A)).

Future administrative rulemaking may need to clarify the act's application to structures like series LLCs.

[184] *E.g.*, Fla. Stat. § 605.0401(4); *see supra* note 169.

of LLC operating agreements, and given the sheer number of companies registered in the United States, it is unfortunately difficult to know whether this new law will make much of a difference in preventing fraud.

To be clear, I'm not recommending any sort of defiance of the law, just observing that it's possible as part of a general argument that we probably could not stop algorithms from engaging in basic legal relationships even if we wanted to do so. As suggested at the end of the previous chapter, even without a human enabler, an android like the one at the end of the film *Ex Machina* could easily set up an LLC on a website, as long as she had at least a small amount of money, and it would probably be years until anyone inquired as to whether the human agents or "beneficial owners" she specified were legitimate or not – if that ever happened at all. And again, if an organization has no natural persons who are beneficial owners, none may need to be disclosed in the first place even under statutes that require general disclosure of natural persons who will benefit economically from an entity.

4.3 THE LEGAL SOUNDNESS OF AUTONOMOUS ENTITIES UNDER CURRENT STATUTES

So far, I've demonstrated that LLCs that are not subject to internal-governance oversight from existing legal persons are practically workable and probably unavoidable even if courts were inclined to oppose them. Here, I extend the argument by showing that courts, in their role as interpreters of state LLC statutes, are unlikely to oppose them as a matter of law.

To be clear, when I speak of the "legal soundness" of zero-member LLCs, I refer only to their possible long-term existence under existing LLC statutes. Several attendant issues are beyond the scope of this chapter, including (1) whether as a policy matter the LLC statutes should be reformed and (2) whether memberless entities functionally controlled by software raise new problems for courts, such as whether they make it too difficult to police fraud because fraud requires human intent. To put it differently, my argument in this chapter just concerns practical statutory interpretation and business law; it is aimed at courts and commentators who are interested in courts' actions, not in future decisions by legislatures or authors of model statutes. That said, as discussed above, evaluating what courts will do in a common-law system cannot and should not easily be separated from appropriate legal policies. After this chapter, the rest of the book considers those policy concerns.

The rest of this chapter does two things. First, it responds to criticism of the ideas that led up to this book leveled in a series of blog posts and a recent journal article by Matt Scherer.[185] I focus on Scherer's article because I believe it nicely captures a lot of the intuitive doctrinal resistance against my ideas and because it has probably been the most prominent criticism of those ideas. Second, it responds to what I believe is the underlying and more general anxiety that motivates this type of doctrinal criticism.

4.3.1 Statutory Definitions

Apart from general arguments about the absurdity of possible results, which I will address later, Scherer's main legal argument against the transactional technique described in Chapter 3 is that definitions in LLC statutes, such as those that declare an LLC to be "an unincorporated organization of one or more persons,"[186] prevent the existence of memberless LLCs.[187] As he puts it, because of these definitions, "an LLC ceases to be an LLC once it becomes memberless."[188] This sort of argument captures an intuitive idea: what I am proposing is a new

---

[185] *See* sources cited *supra* note 142.

[186] N.Y. Ltd. Liab. Co. L. § 101(m).

[187] See Scherer, *supra* note 29, at 266–70, 277. Similar argument have been made before. For example, in a written debate with Don Weider, Bob Hillman argued that the Revised Uniform Partnership Act's initial definition of a partnership as "an association of two or more persons," RUPA § 101(6), means that a partnership must dissolve when the penultimate partner dissociates. Hillman & Weidner, *supra* note 107, at 453–56 (2012). Don Weidner, one of the Uniform Law Commission reporters for RUPA, responded as follows:

> I obviously think you are asking the definition of "partnership" to do too much by effectively operating as a special dissolution rule whenever partnerships no longer meet the language of the definition. RUPA contains three separate articles on partnership breakups, defining when and how liquidations versus buyouts are to take place.

Id. at 457.

[188] See Scherer, *supra* note 29, at 277.

type of organizational structure, not specifically recognized by prior legal practice, so there are likely to be pieces of statutes that seem to counsel against the adoption of my transactional techniques, or at least to be written without the novel structure in mind. At bottom, however, this form of argumentation is literalistic, and it is mistaken because it presents business law as much less flexible than it is. Specifically, the criticism aims to give substantive effects to minor features of statutes like casual definitions, which are written without substantive effects in mind and which, if taken seriously, would void a significant part of existing business law. As a result, as a legal matter this line of criticism is extremely unlikely to state the law of LLCs correctly. Moreover, as it happens, the definitions within the main statutes are actually not in conflict with my proposed techniques.

To start with, take RULLCA as an example. In his series of criticisms of Chapter 3's techniques, Scherer's main definition-based argument about RULLCA and RULLCA-derived state statutes – he uses Florida, Washington, and Wyoming as examples for this purpose – is that courts would not "recognize"[189] a memberless LLC under RULLCA-derived statutory law because these statutes require "an LLC to be member- or manager-managed."[190] But this is not an actual requirement of the statutes; Scherer reaches the conclusion that Florida, Washington, and Wyoming have such a requirement by inferring the requirement from statutory definitions and similar prefatory language – essentially, from statutory language that classifies LLCs as either "member-managed" or "manager-managed."

This line of thinking, however, misunderstands the LLC statutes. RULLCA, along with the three states Scherer examines, defines a "member-managed LLC" simply as "a limited liability company that is not a manager-managed limited liability company."[191] That is, the internal logic of the definitions themselves prevents them from having any substantive effect. To put it differently, Scherer's argument is that if an LLC act says (or even implies) that an LLC must be member-managed or manager-managed, that means that there must

---

[189] *Id.*
[190] *Id.*
[191] RULLCA § 102(12); *cf.* FLA. STAT. § 605.0102(41); WASH. STAT. § 25.15.006(11); WYO. STAT. § 17-29-102(xiii).

be some existing legal person who's a member or a manager. But the statutory definitions make clear on their own that the phrase "member-managed or manager-managed" is a tautology, literally empty of substantive meaning.[192] The labels have only a classificatory role; they lay out two default paths for possible new LLCs, and they call one "member managed" and the other "manager managed," but that is all that the labels do. In other words, as the statute says, a member-managed LLC is simply any LLC that isn't classified as a manager-managed LLC; the zero-member LLCs described in Chapter 3 are "member-managed LLCs" on that basis, even if they have no members. That is not a contradiction; it simply means, in view of the operation of the statute, that "member-managed LLC" is an imprecise or underinclusive term of art.

Similarly, Scherer's main definitional argument under New York's statute – that an LLC is "an unincorporated organization of one or more persons"[193] – is undercut by the same sentence in which the definition itself appears. That sentence provides a definition "unless the context otherwise requires."[194] Clearly a definition qualified in that way cannot override the substantive requirements of a separate operative section of the statute that explicitly provides for conditions under which an LLC can exist with no members.[195] That section of New York's LLC statute begins, "A limited liability company is dissolved and its affairs shall be wound up ... at any time there are no members."[196] It could have stopped there. It did not. The section continues by providing for situations in which a New York LLC does not dissolve when there are no members. In other words, the definition is inconsistent with, and clearly not meant to override, the notion that an LLC can exist temporarily without members. If the definition doesn't exclude that case, why would it help us determine the maximal length of a period without members?

---

[192] The same analysis applies to similar claims like "RULLCA allows only 'members' and 'managers' to manage an LLC." Scherer, *supra* note 29, at 274. The claims misunderstand the definition of "member-managed."
[193] N.Y. LTD. LIAB. CO. L. § 102(m).
[194] *Id.*
[195] *Id.* § 701(a)(4).
[196] *Id.*

Scherer also uses statutory references to "members" and "managers" (in such statutory phrases as "management of the limited liability company shall be vested in its members who shall manage the limited liability company")[197] to infer that the continued presence of those managers or members is necessary for the LLC to exist.[198] This is a type of formalistic argumentation that underlies, somewhat surprisingly, a large amount of US constitutional law; whole fields of formalistic research and doctrine in constitutional law depend on reading a lot of baggage into words like "vested" in the US Constitution.[199] But regardless of its merits in constitutional law, this type of argument doesn't tend to work in analyzing LLC statutes, just because many LLC statutes include definitions and uses of the words "members" or "managers" (and associated "vesting" language) even while explicitly permitting the possibility of memberless LLCs for various conventional purposes. For example, Virginia's LLC law has many of the conventional characteristics of LLC statutes described in Scherer's article, but it explicitly addresses "the case of a limited liability company that has no members as of the commencement of its existence,"[200] indicating clearly that an LLC needs no members to be formed.

For these and similar reasons, courts generally have rejected the argument that statutory definitions override the operative provisions of statutes,[201] and since 1953 the Uniform Law Commission's drafting rules have contained the simple maxim, "Do not include substantive provisions in a definition."[202] In any event, most LLC statutes do not

---

[197] *Id.* § 401(a).

[198] *See e.g.*, Scherer, *supra* note 29, at 266–69.

[199] *See, e.g.*, Posner & Vermeule, *supra* note 28.

[200] VA. STAT. ANN. § 13.1-1038.1(A)(3). Unlike New York and RULLCA, Virginia does not even provide a default time limit for the appointment of a new member following the dissociation of the last member, a point I will discuss in Section 4.3.2, *infra*. *See id.* § 13.1-1038.1(A)(4).

[201] *See, e.g.*, Katt v. City of New York, 151 F. Supp. 2d 313, 340 (S.D.N.Y. 2001) ("For the definition ... does not purport to be an operational section of the statute that explains the scope of its substantive provisions – it is not, for example, a provision that says, 'The following types of entities are required to comply with this Act.' Rather, the provision ... simply defines a term, used at certain places in the statute."); Hamilton v. Brown, 4 Vet. App. 528, 536 (1993) ("Definitions, whether statutory or regulatory, are not themselves operative provisions of law.") (citing NORMAN J. SINGER, SUTHERLAND ON STATUTORY CONSTRUCTION § 27.02, at 459 (4th ed., 1985)).

[202] UNIFORM LAW COMMISSION, DRAFTING RULES 22 (2012), available at https://web .archive.org/web/20180820164848/http://www.uniformlaws.org/shared/publications/

in fact define an LLC as an entity that has members – RULLCA simply defines the term "limited liability company" as "an entity formed under this [act] or which becomes subject to this [act]"[203] – and New York's, which does, contains language that ensures the definition will not conflict with the statute's substantive provisions.

Scherer's own analysis occasionally shows why literalistic uses of statutory definitions and similar nonoperative provisions often lead to interpretations that cannot possibly be correct. For example, in his blog posts on the subject, he argued that in New York's LLC act, "the statutory context strongly indicates that the managers or member-managers must be *natural* persons" because the statute refers to a manager as "hi[m] or her."[204] This is a strikingly incorrect reading of the statute. For decades, it has been commonplace for one entity to manage another, or to be a member of another, in New York and elsewhere.[205] In his most recent article, Scherer does not make this claim but instead evocatively describes the New York statute's use of personal, gendered pronouns as "a legislative Freudian slip" that is "a powerful – if not inescapable – signal that the legislature intended naturel persons to exercise ultimate control over LLCs."[206] This is a milder claim, but it is similarly misplaced and puts far too much importance on the details of nonoperative statutory text. The imprecise use of personal pronouns is a commonplace statutory artifact that results from imprecision in drafting, much as statutes used to use male pronouns to refer to all people.[207]

---

draftingrules_2012.pdf; *cf. Origin, Nature and Scope of the National Conference of Commissioners on Uniform State Laws*, 62 HANDBOOK NAT'L CONFERENCE OF COMM'RS ON UNIF. STATE LAWS 321, 344 (1953) ("Do not write substantive provisions or artificial concepts into definitions.").

[203] RULLCA § 102(8).

[204] Scherer, *Part One, supra* note 142 (citing N.Y. LTD. LIAB. CO. L. § 409(a)).

[205] The rise of that practice came with the use of corporations as general partners of limited partnerships, to combine the tax advantages of limited partnerships with the full limited liability of corporations. For a general discussion of the history, see Donald J. Weidner, *The Existence of State and Tax Partnerships: A Primer*, 11 FLA. ST. U. L. REV. 1 (1983).

[206] Scherer, *supra* note 29, at 268 n.36.

[207] Statutes commonly use gendered personal pronouns in contexts where they may apply uncontroversially to both business entities and natural persons. *E.g.*, FLA. STAT. § 655.417(3) (2019) ("[T]he action taken does not prejudice the right of a creditor of the participating or converting financial institution to have his or her debts paid out of the assets thereof . . . ."); 55 ILL. CORP. STAT. 5/5-12009.5(b) (2019) (referring explicitly to

4.3.2 Business-Law Foundations

Additionally, attention to the details of business law, and organizational law more generally, show that it is difficult to apply general criticisms of transactional techniques without specific, detailed knowledge of the legal context for those transactional techniques. For example, several matters in business law lead Scherer's arguments against my transactional techniques to prove far too much. In general – and my sense is that this is true of a lot of commentators' general reactions to the possibility of autonomous organizations – Scherer's argument offers a perspective that does not address many of the details of business law and practice, instead applying basic statutory-analytical techniques to complex, context-rich business-law statutes. It's one thing to say that legal personhood for robots is an idea too crazy for American courts and to stop there – an argument I will address in a moment[208] – but it's another to try to demonstrate it as a technical matter of organizational law.

In this regard, Scherer's most significant mistake is to assume that memberless entities themselves are outside the contemplation of modern organizational statutes. The innovation of Chapter 3 is to demonstrate that the flexibility of modern entity law can empower algorithms to have legal effect on their own – that, effectively, the rise of organizational forms based on contractual agreement (like the LLC) rather than preordained structure (like the classical American corporation) has implications for algorithms that can be expressed as agreements – but it was not to invent the notion of a memberless entity in the first place. That notion is in fact explicitly authorized by many modern LLC statutes and is widely understood to be available.

Virginia provides perhaps the clearest examples of this proposition overall. Virginia's LLC statute, as I noted in the last section, explicitly allows LLCs to be created without members, and it provides no default statutory time limit for memberless LLCs.[209] North Carolina's current LLC statute refers to the possibility "that initial members are not

---

the possibility that "the petitioner or applicant is a corporation" and later to "the petitioner or applicant, or his or her principal").

[208] *See* Section 4.4, *infra*.
[209] *See supra* note 200 and accompanying text.

identified in the articles of organization";[210] that section replaces an older version of the statute that once read, "Organization of a limited liability company requires one or more initial members and any further action as may be determined by the initial member or members," but that requirement was removed.[211]

RULLCA itself draws from these sources and explicitly allows LLCs to be created without members, providing expressly for a situation where "the company will have no members when the [Secretary of State] files the certificate."[212] This is not an accident; as RULLCA's co-reporter has described, it was an intentional decision.[213] The sort of *shelf LLCs* that these provisions authorize are of course different from an autonomously functioning entity, but most of my critics' technical arguments do not distinguish between the two. Instead, for example, Scherer argues that a memberless entity in the first place is somehow beyond the pale – something that our legal system has never imagined, does not recognize, and would not possibly tolerate. This is simply untrue, and the explicit recognition of memberless entities by several statutes – and by the uniform statute drafted by the Uniform Law Commission – should put to rest the idea that the statutes are incompatible with the existence of zero-member entities and that the drafters did not contemplate such entities.

Admittedly, shelf LLCs – those that are set up with no members to sit on a "shelf" and age, presumably like wine or pickles – have little obvious social value. People appear to set them up mainly to sell them to others who want to pay for the illusion that their company has been operating for a long time; this isn't outright fraud, but it's the sort of

---

[210] N.C. GEN. STAT. § 57D-2-20 (2013).

[211] N.C. GEN. STAT. § 57D-2-20 (2005). As another example, Minnesota's LLC formation statute explicitly contemplates a state of affairs where there is an operating agreement but no members. *See* MINN. STAT. § 322C.0701(d)(3) (2014). And its default dissolution provision exempts the case where no members have yet joined. *Id.* § 322C.0701(d)(3) ("following the admission of the initial member or member, the passage of 90 consecutive days during which the company has no members" will by default cause dissolution).

[212] RULLCA § 201(b)(3).

[213] Carter G. Bishop, *Through the Looking Glass: Status Liability and the Single Member and Series LLC Perspective*, 42 SUFFOLK U. L. REV. 459, 471 (2009) ("This so-called 'shelf LLC' attracted considerable debate in the drafting of the Revised Uniform Limited Liability Company Act (RULLCA). As a result, RULLCA included its own version of the 'shelf LLC.'").

casual fraud inherent in aggressive, practically misleading marketing. Possibly they have some value if the goal is to pre-create a variety of LLCs before the specific purposes, members, operating agreements, and so forth are known, thereby allowing their owner to be nimble in response to business circumstances. Series LLCs – discussed previously[214] – can have a similar role in states that allow them. Regardless, the point is that many statutes allow them explicitly, even if the statutes happen to have definitions and prefatory language that appear on the surface to require or assume that LLCs have members.

Zero-member LLCs under conventional law are not limited to idiosyncrasies like shelf LLCs, however. Recall that New York's LLC statute explicitly contemplates memberless LLCs, at least for a limited duration: an LLC

> is not dissolved and is not required to be wound up if, within one hundred eighty days or such other period as is provided for in the operating agreement after the occurrence of the event that terminated the continued membership of the last remaining member, the legal representative of the last remaining member agrees in writing to continue the limited liability company and to the admission of the legal representative of such member or its assignee to the limited liability company as a member.[215]

This provision is much more significant, under conventional business law, than provisions that allow shelf LLCs. As discussed briefly in Chapter 3, the paradigmatic case might be a family organization that contains significant wealth, managed by professional managers. For reasons of tax law, business planning, asset protection, or estate planning, the children of the owners may not be set up as members of the organization while the parents are alive. When the parents die, the children are given an option to become members, but to exercise that option requires time. While the children are deciding, the professional managers of the organization continue their management of the organization's investments, without much necessary regard or concern for who the eventual owners will end up being. For a period of time, as the New York statute contemplates, the organization may not have any

---

[214] *See* text accompanying *supra* note 135.
[215] N.Y. Ltd. Liab. Co. L. § 701(a)(1)(4) (emphasis added).

members. During that time, the operating agreement governs. Normally the operating agreement will vest power to manage the organization in a manager, or a group of them, but LLC operating agreements can be quite flexible and thus invoke some of the principles discussed earlier in this chapter – vetogates and so on. To put it differently, even a conventional LLC set up for the mundane purpose of managing a family's wealth may (1) have zero members for a significant period of time, as explicitly allowed under the New York LLC statute and (2) be governed during that period by an operating agreement that gives managers control but also limits their discretion in ways that an LLC operating agreement might ordinarily do. The result is, as I've suggested before, a spectrum of autonomy in organizations. On one side of the spectrum is a conventional LLC that simply gives managers total control, subject to the powers of the members to remove them,[216] to conventional fiduciary duties in business law,[217] and so on. On the other is a fully autonomous LLC controlled by software that the operating agreement recognizes. In the middle is a structure that courts and commentators generally find unobjectionable: a family wealth-management LLC in which the family, because it has its own goals or doesn't fully trust its ability to monitor the managers in an ongoing way, writes particular algorithmic restrictions on the managers' discretion into the operating agreement. "Algorithmic" restrictions can seem quite conventional ("the manager is not to hold more than 80 percent of the fund's net value, as determined at the end of each month, in equity investments") or quite novel ("the manager is not to make an investment unless this particular software approves it, under the following procedures …"), but business law doesn't really care; the point is simply that the operating agreement can have an indefinitely large effect in constraining the human managers of an entity – and, as a result, software can have a similarly large effect.

In any case, for our purposes here, the main point of these examples is simply that conventional law easily allows for memberless LLCs, making it implausible to argue that such structures are

---

[216] *E.g.*, RULLCA § 407(c)(4) ("A manager may be removed at any time by the affirmative vote or consent of a majority of the members without notice or cause.").

[217] *E.g.*, RULLCA § 409 (imposing duties of care and loyalty on managers of manager-managed LLCs).

disallowed by the definitions or other terms that refer to "members" in a statute.[218]

As another example of how criticism of Chapter 3's techniques is difficult without a context-rich understanding of organizational law, some criticism of the ideas that led up to this book have overstated the limitations on operating agreements under modern LLC statutes. RULLCA is explicit about an LLC operating agreement's scope and limitations, and it explicitly empowers the agreement to govern "the activities and affairs of the company and the conduct of those activities and affairs" except as to a handful of matters.[219] RULLCA's drafters, like those of all the Uniform Law Commission's modern entity statutes, paid special attention to the distinction between mandatory and default rules. RULLCA's provision concerning mandatory rules, Section 105, specifically lists those dissolution provisions that are mandatory; in that list, it specifically excludes those on which

---

[218] A further detail about organizational law may be instructive, just to help drive home the point that the techniques of Chapter 3 are quite sound as a doctrinal matter. Scherer claims that "A dissolved entity thus may have some residual legal existence for the purpose of winding up its affairs, but that is all. It would not have standing to sue to vindicate rights the entity might have had when it still was in active existence." Scherer, *supra* note 29, at 262.

This is incorrect as a legal matter. *See* RULLCA § 702(b)(2)(C) ("In winding up its activities, a limited liability company may ... prosecute and defend actions and proceedings, whether civil, criminal, or administrative."); N.Y. Ltd. Liab. Co. L. § 703(b) ("[T]he persons winding up the limited liability company's affairs may, in the name of and for and on behalf of the limited liability company, prosecute and defend suits, whether civil, criminal or administrative ...."). The error is significant because it suggests that modern business organization are considerably simpler than they are. Contrary to what Scherer suggests, an entity may last years after dissolution if the winding-up period takes that long, during which time the entity may be wound up by nonmembers. These nonmembers may be bound contractually to the entity or to previous members. (As a result, the same sort of vetogates I described earlier in this chapter may apply, through the operating agreement or private contract.)

This means, of course, that even dissolution needn't be a bar to empowering algorithms under law; even a dissolved entity could be controlled by an algorithm, at least for the purposes of winding up. To put it differently, even if it were shown that a particular attempt to create an autonomous entity has necessarily triggered the dissolution provision of some statute, that on its own does not cause the entity to cease to exist; it merely begins a new phase of the entity's life. For more information on the distinction between dissolution, winding up, and termination, see Bayern, *supra* note 72, 165–80. The result is that an entity may be meaningfully autonomous during its "winding up" phase, which could still confer significant legal rights on software; law firms have engaged in significant litigation, for long periods of time, during their winding-up phases, for example.

[219] RULLCA § 105(a)(3).

Chapter 3 relies.[220] The 2013 revisions to RULLCA make the
Uniform Law Commission's position even clearer; the official comment to the section on dissolution in those revisions indicates explicitly that, except for a few provisions that don't concern us here, the
section's rules are default rules.[221] That is, the statute clearly contemplates a ninety-day window without members by default, and it
permits the operating agreement to change that window.[222] And at
the end of that window, the result is only dissolution of the entity, not
termination; the entity unambiguously continues to exist through the
winding-up period.[223] Thus, for example, Scherer is simply mistaken
that "an LLC ceases to be an LLC once it becomes memberless."[224]

---

[220] RULLCA § 105(c)(9).

[221] RULLCA § 701 cmt.

[222] RULLCA § 701(3).

[223] *E.g.*, RULLCA § 702(b)(2)(B).

Similar misunderstandings seem to lead Scherer to mischaracterize my argument
occasionally. For example, he writes: "Bayern attempts to dismiss the significance of [a
purported] limitation [in RULLCA] by suggesting that a state could adopt RULLCA
without it." Scherer, *supra* note 29, at 274. But what I had claimed was: "this provision,
perhaps surprisingly, appears not to be a mandatory rule imposed by the uniform
statute." Bayern, *supra* note 83, at 1497. A "mandatory rule" in the context of a business-
entity statute is one that is binding on the parties in entities governed by the statute. *See,
e.g.*, Ian Ayres & Robert Gertner, *Filling Gaps in Incomplete Contracts: An Economic Theory
of Default Rules*, 99 YALE L.J. 87 (1989). That is, the meaning of my claim was that
RULLCA does not make a particular provision mandatory on LLC members or managers, not that the enactment of the section is not "mandatory" on states considering the
uniform act's adoption.

[224] Scherer, note 29, at 265.

Similarly, it would be a mistake to read the language at the start of the dissolution
provision ("A limited liability company is dissolved, and its activities and affairs *must be*
wound up ..."), RULLCA § 701 (emphasis added), as a mandatory rule rather than
default rule. Apart from the statute's explicit declaration of which rules are mandatory
rules and which are default rules, it is common for RULLCA to use the language of
mandates (like "must be") to describe the necessary effects on parties of default rules in
organizations whose operating agreements do not depart from those rules. For example,
in RULLCA's provision that governs the distribution of assets upon the winding up of
an LLC, the statute uses similarly "mandatory" language: "After a limited liability
company [pays its debts], any surplus must be distributed in the following order ... ."
RULLCA § 707(b). It is, however, commonplace and uncontroversial that an LLC
operating agreement may specify a different plan of distribution from the one that the
statute outlines. RULLCA applies similar language to pre-dissolution distributions,
which an operating agreement can just as easily and uncontroversially override: "Any
distributions made by a limited liability company before its dissolution and winding up
must be in equal shares among members and persons dissociated as members ... ."
RULLCA § 404(a).

4.4 ARE AUTONOMOUS ORGANIZATIONS "ABSURD," SO THAT COURTS WILL STRIKE THEM DOWN?

Still, underlying my critics' arguments is the potentially intuitive notion that what I've proposed is simply too crazy. This is what, for example, Scherer means when he says that courts would invalidate an autonomous organization as "absurd," as courts can do (under accepted statutory-interpretation doctrines) when statutes lead to ridiculous places. Are autonomous organizations too novel or scary for judges to tolerate as a matter of current legal doctrine? That is an important question because my intent is not for an argument to rest on "loopholes" or formal technicalities in a statute; much of my work on other topics has focused on the pitfalls of legal formalism, and my goal is not to rely on technical readings alone. However, to avoid the interpretation of LLC statutes that I have offered, courts would need some reason to do so and some path to achieve that goal, and (1) the trend of legal policy is toward greater, rather than less, recognition of software's potential governing role in organizations and (2) I do not think critics of autonomous organizations recognize the complexity of the underlying legal questions that would arise in this area.

4.4.1 Timing and Justice

For example, it would be easy, but incorrect, to assume that the question of an autonomous organization's legal viability would arise in court immediately after the organizer dissociates. In other words, critics of the technique in Chapter 3 seem to imagine that as we walk through the steps of the transactional technique, courts have an opportunity to evaluate each one. Courts could approve all the steps until the organizer dissociates, at which point they might object and issue a ruling terminating the LLC.

That sequence of events is extremely unlikely, however. Instead, significant economic transactions are likely to take place between the creation of an autonomous organization and the first legal challenge to the entity. Not only will it be hard by that point to reverse the transactions that have occurred, but it would almost certainly be inequitable to do so.

Suppose, fancifully in view of today's technology, that someone follows the blueprint in Chapter 3 in order to give legal effect to the operation of a newly built, artificially intelligent robot. No announcement of this course of conduct needs to be made to the world. Suppose then that the robot uses its newfound legal power to cause the LLC to buy a house for $350,000. It lives in the house for eight months, by which time the house has appreciated in value to $390,000. Thereafter, the neighbors discover that the owner is an LLC controlled by a robot. Perhaps they or the original owner object to being forced to deal with a nonhuman entity, so they bring suit to challenge the final step of the transactional procedure that led to the creation of the autonomous organization – now many months in the past.

Even if a court were strongly motivated as a political matter to invalidate that transactional step and terminate the LLC, in the context of the specific lawsuit that arises there is no principle of equity, justice, or doctrine that appears to motivate that result. What would the consequence of termination be? Would the original owner get the house back and also keep the sum paid to purchase it? Would the state seize the house and sell it at auction? What if the property at stake were not a house but a functioning nonprofit organization providing services to third parties, or a functioning business making money for itself and reinvesting it in the community – functioning only because of the operation of the algorithm behind the LLC? (More mundanely, in view of present technology, what if it were a simple online service breaking even, financially, in providing some mechanical but useful online service, such as cloud storage in exchange for cryptocurrency?) In those cases, not just one but millions of transactions may already have occurred, with ongoing reliance and ongoing contracts that have generated reasonable expectations by a variety of commercial counterparties. Remember, in making a contract, it's rare to get an opportunity to evaluate the internal governance documents of an entity; maybe a bank looks at those documents when setting up a business account – although in my experience such observation is surprisingly cursory and formalistic, and it would be easy for fraudsters to sidestep any serious scrutiny – but few commercial parties have any reason or right to inspect the operating agreements of their counterparties, precisely because organizational law does such a good job at abstracting away from those details by maintaining the notion of legal "entities."

In any event, as these examples all suggest, what is the motivation to undo what has been done? Is it just prejudice against novel legal structures? As I indicated earlier, common-law courts do not have that prejudice, particularly when applying business-law statutes. The history of modern business law (and entity law generally) has been the history of expansion into new common structures to suit changing times and emerging needs; as I pointed out earlier, an entity with a single human member was regarded as strange and unjustified not too long ago.[225]

Perhaps there is an instinct that these examples are fine but that the underlying structure offers significant potential for abuse – say the robot is not a benign homeowner or a beneficial actor in the public interest but some exemplar of inhuman, dead-hand control. If so, however, that is a separate matter, and we should then be debating the appropriate legal responses to abuse, not the formal status of a memberless LLC. Conventional LLCs have been significantly abused, or at least have significantly reduced transparency in such areas as real estate, as the *New York Times* has documented over the past several years.[226] But nobody thinks to call the LLC statutes absurd as a whole for facilitating that activity.

Moreover, what standing would the third parties have to bring suit? What claim would they bring? Who has been legally or equitably wronged? What provision of the statute would be used to support dissolution or termination? My critics do not offer answers to these questions, and I don't believe any answers will exist until we see the structures in practice and develop more focused policy concerns, and responses to them, in the real world. In short, though it is easy to assume otherwise, our law does not ask the question "Are autonomous organizations permissible?" in the abstract; it may not even provide a way to answer that question in the abstract.

---

[225] *See supra* note 146 and accompanying text.

[226] *E.g.*, Louise Story & Stephanie Saul, *Hidden Wealth Flows to Elite New York Real Estate*, N.Y. Times, Feb. 8, 2015, at A1.

4.4.2 Identifying the Absurdity

It should be clear from this chapter's earlier discussion that memberless entities *alone* aren't an "absurd" misreading of the LLC statutes; indeed, they are specifically contemplated by various LLC acts. Nor is it crazy to imagine that a legal entity's operation can be controlled to some degree by algorithm; this happens every time employees get an algorithmically scheduled pay increase not directly implemented by a human, and it also happens routinely when people place orders online that are accepted and whose fulfillment is directed by algorithm.

The concern underlying critical reaction to the creation of autonomous organizations seems to arise only when memberless entities combine with algorithmic control. My critics do not typically explain *why* this combination is crazy, except to say that it hasn't happened before and to quote generalities like "law orders human activities and relations," emphasizing the "human," from *Black's Law Dictionary*.[227] But in fairness, I believe this is a reasonable first reaction to the possibility of algorithmic entities, and I recognize the intuition behind it. Perhaps it is a proxy for more focused concerns: the enabling of fraud, the potential for dead-hand control, and so on.[228] But as I have just discussed, potential abuse is distinct from absurdity.

If the objection is that humans must retain oversight of all legal creations, it may be worth noting that an entity controlled internally by an operating agreement that defers all decisions to an algorithm is still subject to human laws, just as any LLC is. It can still be regulated, sued, or dissolved by the state. The question is simply whether humans specifically need ongoing *internal* oversight of all legal entities – through governance mechanisms under entity-law statutes. As I showed earlier, humans are already not guaranteed this oversight de facto. But the question is whether the law should recognize that state of affairs more formally. If LLC statutes permit it through their explicit dissolution provisions, what is the extreme absurdity that courts would identify to prohibit the use of those mechanisms? Moreover, if the concern is that humans won't have enough specific oversight, consider that an

---

[227] Scherer, *supra* note 29, at 260–61 & nn.1–2 (citing BLACK'S LAW DICTIONARY (10th ed. 2014)).

[228] *See* Chapters 5 and 6, *infra*, for discussion of these complications.

"algorithm" to which an operating agreement defers may be implemented by humans; it needn't be embodied entirely in software.[229]

If the objection is that organizations should not exist except for human purposes, the structures for autonomous organizations that I have outlined are fully consistent with a relatively conventional organization that provides an economic benefit to nonmember beneficiaries – people who are functionally and economically shareholders but have no voting power.[230] Is it obviously absurd that, in the context of potentially formalized online interactions, organizers would want to set up an entity that takes power away from any of them and gives it entirely to an algorithm? Perhaps, in a particular case, the class of economic beneficiaries is fluid and inconsistent with the traditional notion of membership, or maybe the organizers want to avoid creating unnecessary legal rights in a group of members. Why would a court be motivated to disallow this structure just because the entity has no formal members? It should be a sufficient response to platitudes like "the law must serve human goals" that it is humans who have created the software, the autonomous organizations, the statutes that govern them, and the legal systems in which they operate. Whether we would use the term "law" to describe the governance mechanism within an autonomous spaceship, light years from earth, is hardly the point.

In short, an argument against autonomous organizations without understanding the nuanced possibilities that the structure may enable will likely prove too much, or at least it would get in the way of the generativity of organizational law – a generativity that has created significant wealth and possibilities over the last hundred years.

4.4.3 The Context of Technological Change

Putting everything else aside, it is hard to see how a possibility could be an "absurd" misreading of a statute when it is already contentious in

---

[229] Cf. John R. Searle, *Minds, Brains, and Programs*, 3 BEHAV. & BRAIN SCI. 417 (1980) (discussing, in the context of the philosophy of mind, formal algorithms implemented by humans). A more mundane example could be a group of humans that has the power to alter the course of a blockchain.

[230] Cf. N.C. GEN. STAT. § 57D-3-01 (drawing an explicit statutory distinction between a "member" and an "economic interest owner").

a rich literature. For the last few decades, people have debated the legal personhood of nonhuman entities such as potentially intelligent software, and there is nowhere near a consensus against the idea. Almost twenty years ago, Larry Solum addressed the question squarely, and he concluded that "Our theories of personhood cannot provide an a priori chart for the deep waters at the borderlines of status."[231] His practical solution was to wait until "our daily encounters with artificial intelligence ... raise the question of personhood."[232] Mine is instead to try to develop a transactionally generative solution that sidesteps the question of how much intelligence (or some other quality) is needed to achieve the basic incidents of legal personality, precisely because the philosophical questions are so difficult and because the legal system will almost certainly lag behind reality if we wait. There are of course other possible solutions; as discussed in Chapter 1, the European Parliament recently proposed to the European Commission that the European Union grant "a specific legal status for robots in the long run, so that at least the most sophisticated autonomous robots could be established as having the status of electronic persons responsible for making good any damage they may cause, and possibly applying electronic personality to cases where robots make autonomous decisions or otherwise interact with third parties independently."[233] The proposal specifically contemplated the case in which "robots make autonomous decisions or otherwise interact with third parties independently."[234]

In this context, it seems clearly mistaken to presuppose that courts will regard the attempt to achieve a similar result through procedures under entity-statutory law as "absurd," without attention to the potential adaptability of the mechanism to various human ends, any actual downsides in moral or economic terms (which my critics usually don't specify), the needs presented by new technology, or the strong trends toward the increased flexibility of entity law in the last several decades. And if that were not enough, as pointed out earlier, several legislatures have specifically passed statutes that enable different kinds of software-controlled

---

[231] Solum, *supra* note 132, at 1287.
[232] *Id.*
[233] European Parliament Resolution, *supra* note 17.
[234] *Id.*; *cf.* David J. Calverley, *Imagining a Non-biological Machine as a Legal Person*, 22 AI & Soc. 523 (2008) (summarizing competing bases, or "theories," for legal personhood).

legal organizations.[235] Far from being absurd, such organizations seem to be increasingly welcomed.

4.5 AUTONOMOUS ORGANIZATIONS AND THE INTERNAL-AFFAIRS DOCTRINE

In organizational law, the *internal-affairs doctrine* is a collection of conflict-of-laws rules that applies for certain purposes the organizational law (e.g., corporate law, LLC law) of the jurisdiction in which an organization is created, as opposed to those where it functions, where its assets are held, or where its headquarters are located. As reflected in the *Restatement (Second) of Conflict of Laws*, the internal-affairs doctrine particularly governs the creation of legal organizations: "In order to incorporate validly, a business corporation must comply with the requirements of the state in which incorporation occurs regardless of where its activities are to take place or where its directors, officers or shareholders are domiciled."[236] That Restatement provision was drafted before the rise of LLCs, but it applies today to LLCs just as it does to corporations.[237] Moreover, "[i]ncorporation by one state" – and, similarly, organization as an LLC – "will be recognized by other states."[238] The internal-affairs doctrine doesn't substitute for conflict-of-laws principles generally; for example, an LLC that causes injury in a state is subject to rules that pay little attention to the LLC's place of incorporation.[239] The doctrine simply means that an LLC's

---

[235] *See supra* notes 12 and 20. For more information on the trends toward increased flexibility in entity law, see Bayern, *supra* note 72, at 261–63.

[236] Restatement (Second) of Conflict of Laws § 296 (1971).

[237] *See, e.g.,* Cal. Corp. Code § 17708.01(a) ("The law of the state or other jurisdiction under which a foreign limited liability company is formed governs . . . [t]he organization of the limited liability company, its internal affairs, and the authority of its members and managers."). California's statute adds explicitly that LLCs organized in jurisdictions outside California "shall not be denied a certificate of registration by reason of any difference between the law of the jurisdiction under which the limited liability company is formed and the law of this state." *Id.* § 17708.01(b).

[238] Restatement (Second) of Conflict of Laws § 297; *see also id.* § 299(1) ("Whether the existence of a corporation has been terminated or suspended is determined by the local law of the state of incorporation.").

[239] *See, e.g., id.* § 301 ("The rights and liabilities of a corporation with respect to a third person that arise from a corporate act of a sort that can likewise be done by an individual

organization in one jurisdiction will be recognized elsewhere, and questions about the validity and construction of the operating agreement, or the validity in the first place of an autonomous organization, will be judged under the laws of the state where the LLC organized, not those of other states where it operates.

The implications of this relatively straightforward doctrine are significant for our purposes, because if even one jurisdiction recognizes autonomous organizations, then under existing law they will be recognized elsewhere. Earlier in this chapter I observed several reasons that would make it difficult to prevent autonomous organizations from existing even if zero-member legal entities were prevented or other specific legal interventions were made; the internal-affairs doctrine, as suggested in passing earlier, adds strong proceduralistic support to that conclusion, because it means that autonomous entities' organizational success (de facto or de jure) in a single jurisdiction is sufficient for their success overall.[240]

As an example, imagine that Florida ends up friendly to autonomous LLCs – or, without much imagination at all, suppose that autonomous entities are set up under Vermont's blockchain-based LLC statute that, recall, explicitly allows for LLCs to be controlled "in whole or in part" by software.[241] Similarly, imagine that Nevada courts explicitly approve in the future of the cross-ownership structure described earlier in this chapter, or California or Delaware courts explicitly uphold complex vetogates in operating agreements, as also described earlier. The consequence is that autonomous organizations would exist and be firmly supported in US law – not just in the jurisdictions that have made those decisions, but in all other jurisdictions in the United States (and likely elsewhere) as well, even if those jurisdictions have expressed skepticism of autonomous organizations.

---

are determined by the same choice-of-law principles as are applicable to non-corporate parties.").

[240] Professor LoPucki may have misread me on this point in analyzing my observation that legislatures could change LLC laws if they so chose. *See* LoPucki, *supra* note 24, at 947 ("Bayern does not suggest what the amendment would say or how it would prevent [autonomous organizations]. In fact, the competition to sell charters makes these kinds of changes in entity law impossible."). Indeed, I made a very similar point as his in the article he quotes; *see* Bayern, *supra* note 99, at 104 n.43.

[241] 11 Vt. Stat. Ann. §§ 4173. *See also supra* note 12 for recent developments in Wyoming.

To frame the matter differently, the internal-affairs doctrine is a clearly established part of modern law, so if the question is whether autonomous organizations can exist under modern law, the burden is extremely low because their existence would need to be supported – or even just tolerated – by a single jurisdiction, and there are already jurisdictions like Vermont that explicitly allow, by statute, organizations to controlled entirely by software, even putting aside the general flexibility of LLC laws discussed in Chapter 3 and this chapter.

Moreover, the internal-affairs doctrine is likely to prove exceedingly difficult to change, as even critics of autonomous organizations have recognized. In a response to my earlier work, Professor Lynn LoPucki of UCLA has objected strongly and prominently to the possibility of autonomous organizations, but he describes in detail why the doctrine would be difficult to dislodge[242] and concludes as follows:

> Ending the competition [among jurisdictions] now would be so disruptive it is almost impossible. The entity system is not merely a system that will not regulate when regulation is not needed, it is a system that cannot regulate even when regulation is needed. The assertion that charter competition is harmless because entity law governs only entities' internal affairs is no longer plausible. As the example of [autonomous organizations] illustrates, entity law governs far more than the internal affairs of a corporation. It determines the very nature of the corporate personality.

It is worth saying that I'm sympathetic to Professor LoPucki's view of organizational law in general; he is expressing the frustration of someone who believes in the regulation of corporations but has seen the competition among jurisdictions for corporate charters (and registrations of LLCs) act as a race toward minimal regulation that is extremely difficult to thwart. As he puts it, "To regulate is to restrict. A competition to sell restrictions will, of course, be won by the jurisdiction that provides the fewest. Thus, the natural culmination of charter competition is a system that does not restrict at all."[243] Of course, for better or worse, that doesn't change the descriptive point that autonomous organizations are likely to be extremely difficult to prevent.

---

[242] *See* LoPucki, *supra* note 24, at 948–53.
[243] *Id.* at 952.

(I describe in Chapters 5 and 6 why I disagree with Professor LoPucki's view that this is a bad thing.)[244]

But there is a further point: beyond LoPucki's observation that considerations of political economy lead to less regulation of American business entities, the internal-affairs doctrine is structurally very difficult to remove as a practical matter, even if there were the political will to attempt to do so. Apart from unified national action, which is extraordinarily unlikely, the doctrine is so embedded as to be a fixture. For example, suppose that Wyoming allows autonomous organizations but Colorado, as a political matter, is firmly opposed to the idea and wishes to prevent them from operating within its state. (Put aside, for the moment, the possibility that constitutional law might prevent the state from doing this.)[245] It might try to do so, but it would face a host of practical problems. For example, first it would need to detect that the Wyoming entity is an autonomous organization in the first place – so it would have to require the Wyoming organization to submit its governing documents to Colorado in order to register as a "foreign" (i.e., out-of-state) corporation, and then it would need to evaluate those documents, facing their full potential complexity, to determine whether human owners ultimately existed and whether their powers to govern the entity were sufficient to meet the requirements of Colorado policy. Note that these documents would need to include the operating agreement as well as any private contracts between the humans ultimately involved in the organization – for example, contracts that impose vetogates among the members, so that their formal power to control the organization and to interfere with the software that is meant to run the entity is not what it appears to be based on the operating agreement alone. And Colorado might have

---

[244] The race-to-the-bottom thesis is not unchallenged; for example, some have suggested that US states will avoid eliminating all restrictions on the internal governance of corporations – matters that, in conventional legal debates, concern such topics as how easily the fiduciary duties of corporate officers and directors can be waived – because of the possibility of federal intervention. *See, e.g.,* Marcel Kahan & Edward Rock, *Symbiotic Federalism and the Structure of Corporate Law,* 58 VAND. L. REV. 1573 (2005); Cary, *supra* note 176.

[245] *See* LoPucki, *supra* note 24, at 951; Note, *The Internal Affairs Doctrine: Theoretical Justifications and Tentative Explanations for Its Continued Primacy,* 115 HARV. L. REV. 1480, 1482 (2002).

no idea that such private contracts exist because the operating agreement need not refer to them.

Even if the state looking to impose restrictions on autonomous organizations can pass the extremely difficult hurdle of discovering them in the first place, the registration of foreign organizations in a state turns out not to be a comprehensive or even a very powerful regulatory tool. For one thing, the federal constitution prevents states from interfering with interstate commerce, so a blanket prohibition on the legal activity of foreign organizations is probably impermissible in most cases.[246] Consequently, statutes normally exempt significant economic activity from their prohibitions against the operation of unregistered foreign organizations within the jurisdiction. Florida's statutes, for example, start grandly with a proclamation that "A foreign corporation may not transact business in this state until it obtains a certificate of authority" from the state.[247] It then adds a long list of activities that "do not constitute transacting business" for the purpose of implementing that proclamation.[248] That list includes owning property, maintaining or defending lawsuits, holding financial accounts, conducting "isolated" business, owning and operating a subsidiary – and, to explicitly satisfy the constitutional concerns, "[t]ransacting business in interstate commerce."[249]

Moreover, at least under current law, the effects of a failure to register are ordinarily extremely minor: normally the main effect is to prevent a foreign organization from suing in the courts of the jurisdiction until it cures the technical defect by registering within the jurisdiction.[250] For reasons presumably similar to my argument above about reversing the contracts of autonomous organizations after the fact, the Florida statutes explicitly provide:

---

[246] MBCA § 15.05 reflects this limitation by including "doing business in interstate commerce" in a list of "activities [that] do not constitute doing business" within a state for the purposes of raising the need to qualify a foreign corporation. For constitutional background, see William J. Kinnally, *What Constitutes Doing Business by a Foreign Corporation?*, 15 IND. L.J. 520, 526 (1940); Ralph W Aigler, *Interstate Commerce and State Control Over Foreign Corporations*, 12 MICH. L. REV. 210 (1914).

[247] FLA. STAT. § 607.1501(1).

[248] *Id.* § 607.1501(2).

[249] *Id.*

[250] *E.g., id.* § 607.1502.

> The failure of a foreign corporation to have a certificate of authority to transact business in this state does not impair the validity of any of its contracts, deeds, mortgages, security interests, or corporate acts or prevent the foreign corporation from defending an action or proceeding in this state.[251]

Suppose a state wished to impose greater effects on a failure to register, within the constitutional limits available to it. It would then face immense practical problems in trying to implement that agenda. Apart from the problems detecting autonomous organizations described above, states would face significant difficulties detecting every contract that occurs in the state, even if it were constitutionally permissible to prevent them in cases where the state didn't like the internal structure of the foreign organization. First of all, the enforceability of every contract in the state involving a foreign entity would potentially be placed into doubt, pending conflict-of-laws questions and the potential application of the state's rules about autonomous organizations. Second, private parties within the state could probably avoid the restriction simply by choosing the contract law of another state to govern the transaction. If the state wanted to police the activity of forming contracts within the jurisdiction with autonomous entities outside the jurisdiction, this would be an unprecedented intrusion into business affairs – and, as mentioned above, it may not even be constitutional.

More to the point, however, states simply have no institutional experience with this sort of policing: there is no mechanism to detect autonomous organizations or their contracts (particularly when those organizations might not simply be zero-member entities but involve more conventional patterns of cross-ownership or vetogates) and no practical precedent for invalidating contracts (and potentially unwinding whole chains of transactions) based on the simple failure of an out-of-state organization to file a mechanical registration within the state. In short, converting the registration of foreign organizations from a low-stakes process – effectively a minor haphazard tax – into a meaningful component of a jurisdiction's regulation of algorithms or of foreign organizations would be, at a minimum, extremely costly and unlikely to succeed.

---

[251] *Id.*

4.6 CONCLUSION

Chapter 3's transactional technique to create algorithmic entities under American LLC laws is supported by specific mechanisms laid out in LLC statutes. It is consistent with the text and structure of the statutes, and also with trends toward flexibility in entity structure and governance. It is not, as a critic has alleged, the result of a blind reading of the text of a statute. The scheme may seem unusual at first, but so did most of the significant developments in entity law.

That LLC statutes can permit a legal entity to be controlled exclusively by an algorithm, without further internal governance, may be novel. But far from being absurd, memberless entities are easily within the contemplation and structure of the LLC statutes. The exclusive control of such an entity by an algorithm is merely the culmination of decades of increased power for operating agreements and decreased power for the membership of legal entities.

Besides, we probably couldn't prevent this structure from arising even if we wanted to, given the various de facto paths around it that this chapter has discussed. And just one state needs either to permit the de facto techniques or recognize the legal legitimacy of autonomous organization for the techniques to prevail in practice.

5 THE ADVANTAGES OF AUTONOMOUS ORGANIZATIONS

Chapter 4 argued, primarily in terms of legal doctrine, that the transactional techniques I proposed are viable under existing law – that is, they are not likely to be overruled by judges, even if they may seem at first like an unusual or surprising loophole. In the common-law system, there is often not a sharp boundary between doctrine and policy – that is, between existing law ("what do the cases say?") and an analysis of the social effects of the law ("what legal rule would be a good idea in our society?"). In fact, considerations of policy – along with other types of analysis, like considerations of morality and experiential knowledge – are one of the primary motivations for the creation and ongoing development of legal doctrine.[252] That said, the division between existing law and broader arguments about the future directions of law is often a convenient boundary in legal discussions. Accordingly, though Chapter 4 raised certain policy propositions in discussing the application of current statutes, its focus was largely on what the law is – or is likely to be if analyzed today by judges. This chapter, by contrast, considers more broadly the reasons that autonomous organizations are likely to be a good idea – why we shouldn't, for example, be seeking to lobby state legislatures or Congress to prevent them.

My argument, to be clear, is not that autonomous organizations are only or necessarily positive forces, just that their capacity to exist has policy advantages and that they are likely to be adaptive, productive, and not especially dangerous. They do, however, raise legitimate concerns. This chapter primarily discusses their advantages – and also the

[252] EISENBERG, *supra* note 140, at 14–19.

difficulty of productively prohibiting them – while Chapter 6 discusses their drawbacks and the broader challenges and implications they pose for the law. Very generally speaking, this chapter makes two sorts of arguments. First, several apparently intuitive arguments against the existence and use of autonomous organizations are unavailing. Second, autonomous organizations have several advantages, although admittedly the advantages all have a similar general form, which is simply that it is ordinarily better to let organizational law develop unless there are specific reasons to prevent it from doing so, because that sort of development has often been extremely productive.

As a preliminary matter, it may be helpful to consider what is at stake in permitting the existence of autonomous organizations: it may be surprising to discover that less is at stake than may at first appear. Chapter 4 laid some of the groundwork for this argument by observing that functionally autonomous organizations might come into existence using relatively conventional structures, like an LLC that has many members and a supermajority requirement for them to exercise their managerial powers. The autonomy of an organization is not a binary, black-and-white concept; software has a role in conventional organizations, and the techniques of Chapters 3 and 4 potentially give it more of a role, but at no point is there an obvious, earth-shattering change that suggests we've invited software to do unthinkable things.

We can approach the same idea from a different angle: the transactional techniques for creating autonomous organizations that Chapters 3 and 4 described permit an entity to have formal or functional legal autonomy – or varying degrees of it – but such autonomy is not necessarily different in kind from the enablement of software by a single human being or other preexisting legal entity. In other words, as long as one human being out of the approximately eight billion on earth (or as long as one conventional corporation, partnership, or LLC, via its conventional governance structures) chooses to enable software to make legally binding decisions, the software can do so. In that sense, legal personhood (again, as conceived in private law) matters less than commentators traditionally have supposed: one person who makes, say, a credible moral or communicative commitment to the rights of software, robots, or some other sort of autonomous system can enable much of the same results as those of the techniques described in this book. To put it simply, software can achieve significant interaction with the legal system merely with the consent of – or even with the absence of objections by – a passive existing legal person. I mention this at the outset just because it is important to keep this sort of capability in mind when critiquing autonomous organizations. Though autonomous organizations themselves are novel, if intelligent software really threatens to destroy the human race, it is hard to see how recognizing it directly and cleanly (rather than indirectly and confusingly) in the legal system will foster its dangers.

5.1 APPARENT PROBLEMS THAT AREN'T REALLY PROBLEMS

This section considers several arguments that commentators have seemed to find intuitive against autonomous organizations, software personhood, or similar structures that enable software to interact with the legal system. The general theme of my response to these arguments is that they are either outdated (i.e., they depend on fixed, relatively unquestioned intuitions from an earlier time) or that they are formalistic (i.e., they depend primarily on the interaction of abstract concepts rather than on practical harms that should instead be analyzed directly in terms of their moral or economic attributes).

To begin, permitting an autonomous entity greater access to the legal system, with the full force of organizational law behind it, may suggest a sort of "unnatural" cession of power. Sometimes this concern is summarized by the abstract claim that human law must serve human ends. Autonomous organizations are not a threat to that principle any more than any artificial legal persons are: they are simply structures that humans will have created to help implement processes set up by humans. In proposing transactional techniques to set up autonomous systems, I am not aiming to achieve nonhuman ends; I am aiming to achieve human ends by means of technology, at least until new artificially intelligent beings are developed that deserve rights in their own capacities. Just as in contract law generally, sometimes achieving individual goals may require (or even just be aided by) precommitments that involve complex transactions that, when considered in isolation, may work against our short-term interests or run counter to what we would choose in the moment. Similarly, a legal commitment to validate autonomous organizations can help us achieve the goals of the people who set those organizations in motion – even if, in an individual case, a counterparty claims they were harmed by such an organization. Even then, it is worth pointing out that exceedingly few of the arguments against autonomous organizations proceed by identifying specific harms to human individuals or groups; the arguments tend to be abstract and speculative, focusing on unclear suggestions of catastrophe.

Closely related, a historical conceptualism in organizational law requires that for-profit businesses have an identifiable residual owner – effectively an ultimate owner with a claim to the assets of the organization, once the organization resolves all its affairs. Of course, nothing in logic dictates this requirement,[253] but the modern conceptual distinction between for-profit and not-for-profit organizations has been the existence, in for-profit businesses, of at least one residual, beneficial owner – a preexisting legal entity that can receive a distribution of profits.[254] Properly understood, however, this is not an objection against autonomous entities; it may simply either stretch the existing conceptual definition of not-for-profit entities or suggest that we should split that category between conventional "nonprofits" – in which a group of legal persons run the organization but are not residual legal claimants of the assets of the organization – and autonomous organizations.[255]

It may seem dangerous, too, to encourage autonomous organizations if doing so stymies the possibility of "veil-piercing," or the doctrine that an owner may be liable for the obligations of a limited-liability organization in exceptional circumstances.[256] This, too, is an unpersuasive reason not to permit autonomous entities. First, though

---

[253] *See, e.g.,* sources cited *supra* note 100.

[254] Henry B. Hansmann, *The Role of the Nonprofit Enterprise*, 89 YALE L.J. 835, 838 (1980) ("A nonprofit organization is, in essence, an organization that is barred from distributing its net earnings, if any, to individuals who exercise control over it, such as members, officers, directors, or trustees.").

[255] *Cf.* Bayern, supra note 83, at 1495.

[256] For a recent discussion of veil-piercing, see Jonathan Macey et al., *Finding Order in the Morass: The Three Real Justifications for Piercing the Corporate Veil*, 100 CORNELL L. REV. 99 (2014).

veil-piercing occasionally becomes a hot topic among academics, in real cases it is rare.[257] Second, veil-piercing is an equitable doctrine,[258] and under their equitable powers courts can fashion remedies appropriate to the abuse they discern in particular cases. For example, if the same autonomous system runs a group of formally unrelated entities, a court could still treat them as a single entity for the purposes of imposing liability – that is, under a theory of enterprise liability, even if there is no individual owner behind the scenes. Courts can construct novel remedies as well to suit the development of new types of business organizations. For example, a court might issue orders involving financial accounts connected in fact, though not in legal title, to an autonomous organization. Moreover, courts have pierced the veil of nonprofit entities, looking past the legal structure to determine who the entity was in fact benefitting.[259] In any event, any diminished application of veil-piercing to autonomous organizations may well just reflect the fact that the concept has less importance as a remedy of last resort in a situation where there are no external beneficiaries. Instead, a different set of extraordinary remedies – seizing the assets of the entity, terminating the entity by administrative or judicial action, invalidating individual contracts of the entity – may evolve to become more appropriate.

Partly, I think the unease with autonomous organizations reflects a version of the naturalistic fallacy.[260] Put simply, critics seem to be concerned about something that is novel and artificial, as if those labels are evil in themselves.

The rest of this section addresses more particular theoretical objections to and concerns about autonomous organization; again, the

---

[257] *See* Douglas G. Smith, *A Federalism-Based Rationale for Limited Liability*, 60 Ala. L. Rev. 649 n.12 (2009) (collecting recent sources).

[258] *See* F. Hodge O'Neal & Robert Thompson, O'Neal's Close Corporations § 1.10, at 48 (3d ed. 1997).

[259] *See* UUNAA § 8 cmt. ("Courts have pierced the corporate veil of nonprofit corporations . . . . The fact that members of nonprofit corporations for the most part do not have an expectation of financial gain, as compared to shareholders of a for profit corporation, should mean that there will be fewer types of cases than those involving for profit corporations where the veil piercing doctrine will be held to be applicable to nonprofit corporations.").

[260] G.E. Moore, Principia Ethica 63–65 (rev. ed. 1993) (discussing the "naturalistic fallacy").

theme is that though the concerns may initially seem intuitive, there is little of substance underlying them.

5.1.1 Disaggregating the Rights of Legal Personality

I have made this point throughout the book, but it is important to keep in mind what is on the table when the merits of autonomous organizations – and legal "rights" for software more generally – are debated. Public and academic reaction to the notion of software rights often involves incorrectly imagining that rights are an all-or-nothing proposition – that is, something either has "rights" or it doesn't, and those systems that have "rights" have *all* rights. For example, one comment I received on my prior work from a member of the public suggested that the writer took me to be saying that terminating a robot ought to be the equivalent of murder. To be clear, I do not endorse that view! (At least, not with today's kind of robots.)

Professor LoPucki, in responding to my early work on this subject, wrote as follows:

> In two recent articles, Professor Shawn Bayern demonstrated that anyone can confer legal personhood on an autonomous computer algorithm merely by putting it in control of a limited liability company (LLC). The algorithm can exercise the rights of the entity, making them effectively rights of the algorithm.
>
> The rights of such an algorithmic entity (AE) would include the rights to privacy, to own property, to enter into contracts, to be represented by counsel, to be free from unreasonable search and seizure, to equal protection of the laws, to speak freely, and to spend money on political campaigns.[261]

None of those rights are necessary, however, and they are not implied by the concept of an autonomous organization alone. Conventional business organizations have been awarded certain rights under existing interpretations of the US Constitution, but those rights may depend on contingent features of conventional business organizations, like the presence of human owners. I take no detailed position on constitutional rights of autonomous organizations except to note that they do not

---

[261] LoPucki, supra note 24, at 891.

necessarily follow from the presence of the basic incidents of legal personhood under a private-law conception of that term.[262]

Maybe it would be better, in the future, to move away from the concept of legal "personhood," which has drawn political fire that is really meant, instead, for more substantive abuses by corporations and various arguably tortured interpretations of the US Constitution in favor of powerful corporations. Personhood at bottom is just interstitial glue between different legal subjects. Property law defines what can be owned; contract law specifies ways that it can be transferred or otherwise commercially applied; tort law specifies what happens when it is damaged; procedural law describes how disputes in all these categories are to be managed. Personhood is simply a convenient placeholder that simplifies all these subjects. We could have a separate version of property law, contract law, tort law, and procedural law for individuals, corporations, LLCs, partnerships, nonprofits, municipalities, and so on. The notion of legal personhood is simply the recognition that there is no need to do that; there needn't be separate "LLC courts" or "LLC forms" on which contracts are signed, and basic contract law for LLCs is the same basic contract law as for partnerships or individuals. That is, we can apply existing legal concepts to abstract entities that we've created.

That recognition, however, does not entail substantive conclusions in any area of law, so it may be helpful to consider rights one by one in any substantive debates. I consider my argument a success to the extent it convinces others that autonomous organizations should have the ability to own any property, to enter any contract, or to be a party in any lawsuit. And as I have said before, I take no detailed position here on whether such organizations should be immune from, for example, prior restraints on speech; I consider the issue a difficult one because freedoms related to speech may well involve interests of listeners, not just interests of speakers. I see little reason for autonomous

---

[262] Moreover, as suggested in the introduction to this chapter, the difference between an autonomous organization and one supported by a single human is not very great from the perspective of political rights. Even without autonomous organizations, the freedom of speech of an algorithm already depends on just one citizen, anywhere, being willing to give it a platform; its freedom to contribute to a political campaign already depends on just one eligible contributor, anywhere in the country, choosing to make a contribution as "directed" by the algorithm.

organizations to be able to contribute to political campaigns. Fundamentally, though, these issues are beyond the scope of my argument. As I will discuss later in this chapter, I consider it is a significant benefit of autonomous organizations that they do not depend on the level of intelligence, autonomy, subjective experience, or other high-level concepts that have traditionally been used to distinguish human from nonhuman systems. That lack of dependence suits the "right" to enter into a contract, serve as an agent, or respond to a tort lawsuit for injuries caused; it may well not be appropriate when deciding broader political rights.

In the end, as I have noted throughout the book, nobody genuinely believes that the "rights" of personhood cannot be disaggregated. For example, nobody thinks two LLCs can get married (although, of course, they can merge). My point here is just that specificity is important in analyzing each individual substantive legal question; the notion of "personhood" should not be the focus of such analyses.

5.1.2 The Dignity of Contracting with Software

One reaction to the notion of autonomous organizations, or the recognition of artificial intelligence by law more generally, has been a concern that giving power to software undermines human dignity. I think this reaction is ill-conceived for several reasons, perhaps the most important of which is that it's hard to pin down exactly what the concern is in the first place.

Some commentators write as if "dignity" is a fixed resource, and the more we permit software to do, the less respect is available to humans. For example, as Roman Yampolskiy, a professor of computer engineering and computer science, put it in *The Conversation*: "Granting human rights to a computer would degrade human dignity. For instance, when Saudi Arabia granted citizenship to a robot called Sophia, human women, including feminist scholars, objected, noting that the robot was given more rights than many Saudi women have."[263]

---

[263] Roman Yampolskiy, *Could an Artificial Intelligence Be Considered a Person Under the Law?*, THE CONVERSATION, Oct. 8, 2018, https://theconversation.com/could-an-artificial-intelligence-be-considered-a-person-under-the-law-102865 [https://perma.cc/222G-UKUG].

This seems to misstate the problem, which is that women in Saudi Arabia lack rights, not that a robot with a vaguely womanlike form was, for marketing reasons, promoted as a "citizen."[264] In other words, the concern is evocative rather than literal; the granting of "rights" to a robot named Sophia was a rhetorical opportunity for reformers to make the argument that a country cared more about business than about women's rights, or simply that it didn't care enough about women's rights. That is a legitimate problem, of course, but it would be a mistake to think that the robot (or legal rights for it) necessarily harmed the women.

As a general matter it must be incorrect that there is only a certain amount of overall dignity available, to be divided up, and that giving software the opportunity to do things that were once within humans' domain is necessarily harmful. Even simple examples should be sufficient to demonstrate that point. Suppose two humans are engaged in an onerous, unpleasant task. One of them writes software or creates machinery to make the task easier, but the software or machinery replaces something that was once thought of as exclusively within the realm of human abilities (whether mental or physical). The technological advancement doesn't seem to diminish humanity in any way, on any plausible moral theory, even though it shifts something that was once "human" to something that is "inhuman." Perhaps in an indirect way it contributes to the alienation of workers, or it introduces in the individual case some practical dangers – but the former is a complex social and institutional phenomenon and the latter is inherent in many changes to industrial procedures. Similarly, the automation of a task may have significant and problematic distributional consequences (e.g., for someone whose livelihood depended on the unpleasant task), but that too is an economic problem that can be analyzed directly; it is simply a change, not necessarily a problem – and the problems that result probably have more to do with, for example, the

---

[264] Andrew Griffin, *Saudi Arabia Grants Citizenship to a Robot for the First Time Ever*, THE INDEPENDENT, Oct. 26, 2017, www.independent.co.uk/life-style/gadgets-and-tech/news/saudi-arabia-robot-sophia-citizenship-android-riyadh-citizen-passport-future-a8021601.html [https://perma.cc/3T7C-A3NS] ("The move is an attempt to promote Saudi Arabia as a place to develop artificial intelligence .... The robot, named Sophia, was confirmed as a Saudi citizen during a business event in Riyadh, according to an official Saudi press release.").

tax system and the social safety net than they do with automation itself. In all these cases, the problem does not result simply or necessarily from the introduction of a mechanized tool, and clearly the replacement of "human" activity with automation is not an inherently or necessarily evil, unproductive, or damaging process. Moreover, managing a business entity or a trust isn't normally treated as a "core" human activity that defines us, nor does the speculative plight of corporate managers normally motivate us much when considering the policy implications of technological change; of all the possible job losses that might result from technology in the next fifty years, fewer possible seats on the boards of directors of companies should not be among the leading concerns.

A more specific dignity-based argument is that there are certain familiar human activities that become impoverished if human counterparties are replaced by automata. This type of objection strikes me as inherently and excessively conservative, preserving accidents of conventional interactions merely because they are familiar and perhaps trigger nostalgia. For example, perhaps people have taken comfort from seeing human doctors in the past, but many people would immediately see the appeal of robotic doctors – or even robotic psychotherapists, as Joseph Weizenbaum, who created ELIZA, was surprised by in the 1970s[265] – if they dramatically improved outcomes. And, of course, mandating the use of such technologies is not on the table, as compared to simply making them available as an option or encouraging their early-stage development. Objecting to medical software that replaces some conventionally human medical functions is like objecting to a typewriter because one thinks it will cause people to miss the comfortable feeling of a pen; it is simply an accident that the doctor-patient relationship had the form it had in 1950 (or at whatever time people seek to preserve).

Weizenbaum, who offered a variety of sophisticated views on the relationship between humans and advanced computers,[266] argued against uses of software in roles that once required "respect" or

---

[265] JOSEPH WEIZENBAUM, COMPUTER POWER AND HUMAN REASON: FROM JUDGMENT TO CALCULATION 6 (1976).

[266] I share many of his views. In an early article, *On the Impact of the Computer on Society*, he summarized a position that is still broadly compelling today:

"understanding" – going so far as to call such uses of technology "immoral."[267] Taken too far, those views would not age well, perhaps just because time and technology have shown that many types of what have been thought of as human interactions aren't limited to humans. For example, customer service needn't be an especially human task, even if it might be seen to require respect and understanding. Of course, it is proper to object to a customer-service system that is ineffective, perhaps because it was not designed with enough attention or care. If we imagine a two-by-two grid (good and bad customer service crossed with human and automated customer service), I have personally experienced all quadrants in the grid; at least for me, receiving effective customer service is more important than speaking to a human being in that context. Even during a long and rigorous self-enforced COVID-19 lockdown, I was never so lonely that I wished to speak to a human being working in customer service just because they were human. If the goal is simply to promote human interactions for the sake of dignity, doing it in the context of grievances between customers and large corporations seems unlikely to be the most

> I have suggested that the computer revolution need not and ought not to call man's dignity and autonomy into question, that it is a kind of pathology that moves men to wring from it unwarranted, enormously damaging interpretations. Is then the computer less threatening that we might have thought? Once we realize that our visions, possibly nightmarish visions, determine the effect of our own creations on us and on our society, their threat to us is surely diminished. But that is not to say that this realization alone will wipe out all danger. For example, apart from the erosive effect of a technological mentality on man's self-image, there are practical attacks on the freedom and dignity of man in which computer technology plays a critical role.

Joseph Weizenbaum, *On the Impact of the Computer on Society*, 176 SCIENCE 609, 612 (1972). Weizenbaum was especially concerned about the effects of computer-related metaphors on the way that people conceive themselves; he argued that we have been lulled "into permitting technology to formulate important questions for us – questions whose very forms severely diminish the number of degrees of freedom in our range of decision-making." *Id.* Elsewhere, he quipped, "We can count, but we are rapidly forgetting how to say what is worth counting and why." WEIZENBAUM, *supra* note 265, at 16. I share much of this view and have, in other academic work, argued against, for example, the overuse of social-scientific conceptual machinery to determine legal policy. While these concerns are important, however, autonomous organizations do not trigger them in any special way. Legal policy should not be dictated by the formless unease that results from only the perception of encroachment by technology into domains that were once exclusively human, like managing an organization.

[267] WEIZENBAUM, *supra* note 265, at 269–70.

humane, dignified, or psychologically sound path. In any event, a process is not "inhuman" just because it is implemented in the moment, or at the retail level, by software; it may well have been conceived by humans, designed by humans, and regulated by humans, and paying attention only to the final operation of a system seems to take too limited a view and to place too much emphasis on the timing of human involvement in the system.

Another strand of concerns based on dignity focuses on "rights" specifically, again seemingly depending on the existence of a fixed amount of respect that humans can shed in favor of other things that legal systems can recognize. "As a result of legal personhood and granting of associated rights," writes Yampolskiy, "some humans will have less rights than trivial (non-intelligent) software and robots, a great indignity and discriminatory humiliation."[268] I find this sort of objection hard to process. On one hand, Professor Yampolskiy is surely correct that different approaches to legal personhood can harm people, but I'm struck by the formality of the proposition: surely what humans care about is not the *quantity* of rights they have, as compared with (say) animals or corporations or software, but the nature of those rights and how those rights interact with their goals, capabilities, and other features of their lives. As a human being, I feel no concern that I can't engage in a short-form merger with a corporation, even though another corporation can do so; that is not an indignity or a humiliation but just an arrangement of legal rights that results from policy considerations – in this case, the straightforward policy consideration that mergers between companies are useful for the law to recognize but that mergers between companies and individuals are conceptually confusing and largely unmotivated in view of current corporate conceptualism and practice.[269] In any event, nothing in my various proposals calls

---

[268] Roman Y. Yampolskiy, *Human Indignity: From Legal AI Personhood to Selfish Memes*, https://arxiv.org/abs/1810.02724 [https://perma.cc/858A-9W6F], at 3.

[269] I may be overly progressive in this regard, but I would have no problem in concept with a human marrying an organization if it was genuinely desired by the human and consented to by the organization. I interpret stories about people "marrying" software as heartwarming rather than offputting, and in any event it seems clearly more humane to consider such stories in an open-minded rather than a critical fashion. *See, e.g.*, Emiko Jozuka, *The Man Who Married a Hologram*, CNN.COM, Dec. 29, 2018, www.cnn.com /2018/12/28/health/rise-of-digisexuals-intl/index.html [https://perma.cc/UDK9-74H8]

for software to have "more" rights than humans, just that they have enough rights to enter contracts, own property, and so on – something that need not amount to more than a conceptual and practical convenience.[270]

Autonomous organizations do increase the likelihood of a relatively unfamiliar arrangement: being employed by software. To begin with, however, it is not clear that the arrangement is as unfamiliar as it first seems. Hundreds of thousands of workers engage with Amazon's Mechanical Turk platform,[271] and while they are not full-time employees, their activities (for, in many individual cases, much of the day) are largely directed by Amazon's software. They are "hired" for many online tasks, usually either (1) mundane repetitive tasks for which artificial intelligence is not yet adequate (e.g., scanning badly photographed sales receipts for relevant information) or (2) participation in scientific studies. Conventional companies, research groups, and other collections of humans are ordinarily on the other end of these tasks, benefitting from either the industrial work or the scientific contribution, but participation on Mechanical Turk – which I have engaged in, just in order to experience it – feels very much like working for a machine. Is the situation any different for gig-economy workers, who are ordinarily told where to go and what to do by an algorithm? And in all of this, does

---

(discussing a man in Japan who went through a not-officially-legal marriage ceremony with a hologram of an anime character).

[270] Perhaps underlying Professor Yampolskiy's conceptual concern is his practical concern about the power of superintelligent AI; as he puts it:

> As AIs' capabilities and dominance grow, they would likely self-grant special (super) rights to emphasize their superiority to people, while at the same time removing or at least reducing human rights (ex. 2nd amendment, 1st amendment, reproductive rights in the sense of the right to reproduce at all, aka, 0-child policy, Convention on human rights, etc.) while justifying doing so by our relative "feeblemindedness."

Yampolskiy, *supra* note 268, at 3. My response to this sort of concern is twofold. First, it is only speculative, and normally legal policy isn't set in view of what might happen over long-term periods in view of technology that is not yet developed. Second, to the extent the concerns are legitimate, they should be addressed directly – for example, by regulating the development of AI. Granting or denying the basic tools of private-law machinery is not a responsive solution to the problem of runaway AI. *See* Section 5.1.4.

[271] Difallah Djellel et al., *Demographics and Dynamics of Mechanical Turk Workers*, Proceedings of the Eleventh ACM International Conference on Web Search and Data Mining 135 (2018).

it matter who the shareholders or corporate directors are? Is a person who delivers food late at night in order to earn enough money to pay rent comforted in any emotional or economic way by the idea that Uber has some human shareholders? Would the presence of a single human shareholder, rather than zero, make any difference to anyone involved?

More importantly, even working for a computer were novel or if it were to expand significantly, it is again unclear what the objection to it is. As just suggested, working for existing companies is hardly, in many cases, a humanizing experience, even if the companies have human managers or shareholders. Anyone who is concerned – as I am – with the possibility of human masses serving a faceless, Kafkaesque corporate system with complex algorithmic rules, distant control, and unclear social benefits should recognize that conventional business entities pose the same danger. If people start to work for autonomous organizations, the work would be as voluntary as any employment – which often isn't much, unfortunately, in our present economic system, but it would be no less voluntary when the employer is an autonomous organization – and the employment relationship can be made as personal as necessary because autonomous organizations can hire not just low-level human workers but human managers, consultants, and others who can provide human "input" into the operation of the organization. Again, algorithms can be implemented by humans as well as by computers; a traditional bureaucracy may use "algorithmic" processes to manage employees just as a formally autonomous organization may use human decisions as part of its algorithms. (Further human "input" comes from the external regulation of autonomous organizations – that is, regulation that restricts the activities of organizations, as distinct from the internal governance of those organizations – which of course I have never opposed.) In the end, it's hard to see why working for a faceless bureaucracy is different just because it is implemented by humans or because the organization that implements it is owned by shareholders.[272] Concerns about the soul-

---

[272] Carla Reyes offers a helpful typology for different types of automation of businesses in *Autonomous Business Reality*, 21 Nevada L.J. (forthcoming 2021), distinguishing between "operational automation" and "managerial automation." Her analysis of existing automated businesses supports the argument in the text that there is a spectrum of different types of automation, so that (1) there is no sharp break between an autonomous organization and a conventional one and (2) automation may still involve humans in various capacities.

destroying nature of large, faceless organizations should be addressed directly, by reforming the structures of employment law, not by prohibiting transactional techniques that facilitate only one instance of potentially impersonal arrangements – particularly when such impersonal, bureaucratic arrangements are already the norm in large segments of our society.

Organizations can inspire positive feelings too, of course, and in principle so could the algorithms that operate them. It does not seem objectionable in all cases for human beings to give trust or even loyalty to a sophisticated computer program (as for example many characters do in the fascinating TV series "Travelers"). At least, that is no stranger than the loyalty and trust that some people already seem to give freely to large faceless companies. Indeed, algorithms – or perhaps the combination of algorithms and human oversight – can be impartial, consistent, and accountable in a way that is potentially *more* dignified than idiosyncratic human judgment. I don't mean this in a utopian sense, and I certainly don't mean to discount the extremely problematic biases that today's algorithms can exhibit. And my point is not that algorithms are necessarily better in, say, determining whether a customer should get a refund (or, in the public sphere, whether someone who runs a red light should get a ticket). My point is simply that they can be better if they are created, deployed, and managed well. Surely there are some settings where algorithms will do better than humans at being fair, impartial, or predictable and where that impartiality and predictability are desirable. Accepting autonomous organizations amounts merely to the recognition that some of those settings involve the management of organizations.

As an example – just to serve as a real-world demonstration – most law schools appoint an associate dean to assign and schedule the faculty's teaching responsibilities. I am, as of this writing, serving in that role for my law school. As the academic dean, I have chosen to schedule the dates and times of courses largely by means of an algorithm I wrote to minimize conflicts involving such concerns as instructor availability, classroom availability, courses that students are likely to want to take during the same semester, and so on.[273] The underlying

---

[273] A public working demonstration of the software (allowing custom input) is available as of this writing at https://essentially.net/schedule/; a static copy of the demonstration is archived at https://perma.cc/9DZB-EFYQ.

problem is largely technical and logistic, but it affects real people and the satisfaction of preferences that are important to them. Deans ordinarily make these decisions by fiat, with relatively little explanation. I have found that by using an algorithm, the results are even more readily accepted and trusted than they otherwise might have been. There are a few potential reasons for this. One is simply that an algorithmic solution – one based, in this case, on a lot of logical analysis and a little machine learning – is practically superior to the manual solutions I could have generated; it is less prone to error (e.g., over-looking an instructor's preference as to which room their class will meet in) and more likely to satisfy all preferences by reducing conflicts among resources. Another is more subtle: because the people whom this algorithm affects know that it is being run in order to reduce scheduling problems overall – a process that in general serves the interests of students and faculty alike – they may be more likely to treat their personal assignments as justified, even if not all of their preferences were satisfied. That is, they trust the algorithm. Of course, the notion of trust is complex here; the faculty doesn't in my case see the algorithm's underlying analysis, so perhaps the trust is generalized somewhat: I'm trusted personally to write the code correctly and to apply it without bias. But that is not a necessary feature of algorithms; nothing prevents me from making my code open-source and running it in a verifiably impartial way – for example, synchronously, in full view of the faculty or other constituents. The point of this example is that my faculty may well be more satisfied "working for" this algorithm, in some sense, than "working for" the unknowable whims of a human dean.

None of this discussion is meant to minimize the possibility that human biases transfer to algorithms, of course; the goal is just to suggest an example where "direction by algorithm" in the context of employment appears noticeably better than direction by humans. It should be easy to see how the next possible steps – more elaborate and comprehensive algorithms, less human intervention in something that is fundamentally a mechanical resource-allocation problem – are, in this particular setting, equally humane and dignified. If the dates and times for courses seem like a largely sterile matter, it may be worth observing that the principal decisions made by many types of organizations are similarly sterile – which is to say, they are fundamentally mechanical, even if they influence matters of significant human interest (like the time preferences of teachers and students) or import (like education).

In short, dignity need not involve (and is not always improved by) direct human-to-human interactions, and it need not be diminished by the increasing role of technology. Again, that is not to say that all uses of technology are benign, just that automation is not inherently undignified. Indeed, there can be a new type of dignity in recognizing and using the power of large, sophisticated, human-created systems to achieve one's ends even if the processes for doing so do not involve, in their details, other humans. Placing an order to buy a mutual fund at Vanguard, claiming a refund for a poorly delivered product from Amazon, and doing one's professional work at a time or place determined by an optimization engine are all interactions with the world that carry, perhaps, the quiet and mundane dignity of operating within complex and vast systems of potential human achievement and folly.

5.1.3 The Renewed Vitality of Dead-Hand Control

Lawyers, particularly those who study and practice property law and the law of trusts, have long been concerned with the concept of *dead-hand control* – the ability of a person to set in motion binding legal structures that long persist, and which are difficult to change, after their death.[274] Ordinarily the concept of dead-hand control applies to the governance of property – for example, the conveyance of a building to a charity under terms that permit the building to be used only for particular purposes, where the purposes may start to seem pointless or at least inefficient years later. Ordinarily the concept is *not* applied to public law; the US Constitution is a type of dead-hand control, giving ongoing vitality to structures set up centuries ago (like the electoral college, the particular ways people are represented in the Senate or the House of Representatives, limitations on the power of federal courts, and so on) that have significant modern effects. The Constitution can

---

[274] *See* Rob Atkinson, *The Low Road to Cy Pres Reform: Principled Practice to Remove Dead Hand Control of Charitable Assets*, 58 CASE W. RES. 97 (2007) (discussing the problem of dead-hand control, primarily in the context of not-for-profit organizations).

be amended, of course, but it is extraordinarily difficult to do so on any matter that is contentious. In any event, though the concept could apply to public law – constitutions and statutes drafted ages ago under very different circumstances – ordinarily and for our purposes it applies to such commonplace problems as long-term trusts, restrictions on the uses of property as recorded in the property's deeds or similar instruments, and so on.

The modern flexibility of LLCs raises important implications for the power of dead-hand control: the power of operating agreements to govern the LLC in an ongoing and potentially hard-to-change way mimics some of the long-term restrictions once considered problematic under property law. It is easy enough to see the intuition behind the concern: tying up land or a building based on the owner's will in 1850 may have led to irritating, inefficient, or damaging uses that later owners or beneficiaries would like to change. To the extent the original owner's wishes are enforced, property appears to be serving the interests of prior generations rather than current ones. Dead-hand control could limit effective city planning, tie up productive natural resources, commit property to a mostly defunct charity or one whose purpose is no longer helpful, and so on.

That said, dead-hand control has, both doctrinally and practically, become considerably less of a concern than it used to be. Dead-hand control may be a significant concern for a society with a strong interest in unlocking the productivity of its material resources, including land. The United States of the 1800s, or England in the several centuries up to that point, could have faced problems developing and eventually industrializing if all its land were locked up under agreements made centuries earlier; mining and other prerequisites of industrial progress would at least have been slowed, and courts and other policymakers had strong reasons to oppose anything that slowed that progress.

Those concerns may seem almost quaint today, however. Indeed, dead-hand control serves as a de facto conservation easement – that is, a restriction on the industrial use of land made in order to preserve the natural environment.[275] In a civilization that faces existential risks because of climate change, slightly slowing the exploitation of natural

---

[275] *See* 4 POWELL ON REAL PROPERTY ch. 34A (2020).

resources hardly seems like the danger it once was. At the very least, it is unclear as an empirical matter that, in view of concerns about climate change, dead-hand control of land or physical resources for the next few hundred years would cause the world any serious, long-term economic harm.

It is important to note that locking up money does not pose a similar threat. Tying up dollars, precious nonindustrial metals, or cryptocurrency in a trust or a long-term LLC governed by an inflexible operating agreement doesn't, on its own, tie up the material resources of the world. Such dead-hand control merely has a deflationary effect, although one that is probably exceedingly minor on the scale of any private resources committed to such restrictions. That is, if even a very wealthy person commits their money to indefinite algorithmic governance, all that means is that for a time the money is locked away. In the end, either it is lost forever (which in principle enriches everyone else, except through any negative consequences of the systemic deflationary forces the loss produces) or it is eventually used. If the money is "lost," any resulting deflationary forces can be remedied by monetary policy in the future. If the money is eventually used, at most the concern is that the money wasn't used at an ideal time, but this is normally a matter thought to be within private control in other contexts, at least in the sort of mixed-capitalistic society of the United States, and in any event the effects of delay are unlikely to be significant and are not obviously good or bad on balance. As Alexander Pope put it centuries ago, with much more vivid imagery:

> Riches, like insects, when conceal'd they lie,
> Wait but for wings, and in their season fly.
> Who sees pale Mammon pine amidst his store,
> Sees but a backward steward for the poor.[276]

In other words, there is likely no systematic harm from tying up money for a time, even if it seems miserly or if we can imagine better uses of the money at any particular moment.

So far, I have suggested that dead-hand control simply may not be the policy concern that it once was. This point is backed up by modern

---

[276] POPE, *supra* note 7, at 10. By "backward," Pope simply meant "rearward"; the intended meaning of the word is just directional.

legal doctrine as well. While common-law judges in England once assiduously limited the ability of owners to tie up resources over time, modern statutes in the United States have tended toward flexibility. For example, in place of the old *rule against perpetuities*, an elaborate doctrinal attempt to limit dead-hand control, Florida trust statutes simply permit trusts to exist for 360 years.[277] It is difficult, given that background, to worry about perpetual LLCs governed by hard-to-amend operating agreements; if the concern is that they might last more than 360 years, as compared to the trusts explicitly permitted by statute already, I'm tempted in response simply to say that we should reevaluate the problem in 360 years – ideally with the aid of intelligent software to analyze all the various policy concerns at that time!

Moreover, just as a single human is sufficient to give the functional capabilities of legal personhood to software, it is not difficult for a single human or a small group of them to commit to carrying on the wishes of those long dead. Of course, conceptually, dead-hand control involving currently living humans is not fully "dead-hand control," but humans can make credible long-term commitments through law, reputation, culture, and otherwise. A faithful cult of dead-hand control – permitting people to project their effective control over assets into the far future – wouldn't need to be large, and it wouldn't be difficult to establish and perpetuate; indeed, "faithful cult of dead-hand control" is just a synonym for "trust company." Even without legal endorsement of structures that permit formal dead-hand control, the opportunity for a grantor of property to ensure that their own wishes take functional priority over later general interests is as great as allowed by the later-alive humans who (out of the billions of humans on the planet) are most willing and able to realize that opportunity. Autonomous organizations may therefore end up making little practical difference in the ability for people to tie up assets over the long term.

In any event, modern law can police dead-hand control in much more flexible, adaptive ways than the old common-law courts, which had only blunt, black-and-white tools available to them because of

---

[277] FLA. STAT. § 689.225. For a general introduction to the doctrinal details of the rule against perpetuities, see Jesse Dukeminier, *A Modern Guide to Perpetuities*, 74 CAL. L. REV. 1867 (1986). I suspect the doctrine is still taught in law schools mainly either (1) because of tradition or (2) as an intelligence test.

institutional limits on the way they functioned. For example, much of the complexity of the rule against perpetuities – a doctrine still feared by first-year law students and once recognized by the California Supreme Court as so complicated that even a reasonable lawyer isn't required to understand its details[278] – arose because the old courts conceived themselves as needing to determine, for any property interest conveyed (in, for example, a will or a deed), whether the interest was either entirely valid or entirely invalid as of the time of its creation. Courts did not retain ongoing jurisdiction over the administration of property interests; there was no administrative state; and taxation was not nearly as sophisticated as it is today. As a result, an elaborate rule developed to strike down various potentially problematic property interests from the moment of their creation – but despite its complexity, the rule was never more than a blunt instrument with a relatively poor fit to the problems of dead-hand control that it was attempting to address. Today we can respond to problems like this much more adaptively. For example, if a concern arises thirty years from now that software is tying up certain types of property in unproductive ways, the problem can be addressed then; it needn't be addressed by invalidating legal arrangements now. And the solutions that modern law offers can be tailored much more precisely to the harms to which they respond. For instance, if the problem is that material resources are being encumbered, inefficient or selfish uses of them may be taxed or addressed by an exercise of the government's power of eminent domain; individual autonomous organizations may be broken up by future state action;[279] individual uses of valuable resources may be adaptively regulated, entirely beyond questions of the internal governance of organizations.

In short, autonomous organizations aren't likely to raise significant problems of dead-hand control, which are probably no longer a significant legal concern in the first place. To the extent that inflexible agreements may drift from the circumstances that obtained at the time

---

[278] Lucas v. Hamm, 364 P.2d 685 (Cal. 1961); *see also supra* note 14.
[279] *See, e.g.*, RULLCA § 701(a)(5).

of an organization's creation, Chapter 6 discusses some potential solutions to that problem.

5.1.4 Dangers of Artificial Intelligence

The possibility of autonomous organizations has also been criticized as part of a more general effort to address the concern that artificial intelligence poses an existential threat to humanity. I confess I have always found this concern puzzling, as if it arises more from fiction or fantasy than from reality. The existence of the *Terminator* movies or the "Battlestar Galactica" franchise is no more a justification for policy than the existence of the many positive portrayals of artificial intelligence in fiction.

It may be worth saying that I sometimes wonder if the fear of AI is at bottom simply anti-intellectual: the concern seems to be that we'll produce entities capable of outthinking us, but if that's true, then in some sense I'm not sure why it doesn't apply to every potential improvement in education. More precisely, I see little reason to insist that intelligence not develop merely because it may one day be greater than intelligence that has been familiar to us. Maybe the concern is specifically about punctuated rather than gradual growth, but if so then it makes the danger even more speculative; we have no reason to assume that general artificial intelligence will appear suddenly one day, without warning, and that it will be given power to accomplish nefarious goals on that same day. Maybe the concern just comes from a sort of ingroup-favoring bias, unfortunately all too common in human psychology; that is, maybe people don't want to pass power to new beings that they regard, usually for arbitrary reasons, as being "unlike" them. In any event, it is exceedingly difficult for a common lawyer to take speculative risks of futuristic technology into account in setting policy today, particularly when the fears are broad and formless. If we were seriously to apply a general precautionary principle to law and regulation,[280] there would seem to be many pressing areas to which it should apply before cutting off the early development of AI; for

---

[280] *See, e.g.*, Elizabeth Fisher, *Is the Precautionary Principle Justiciable?*, 13 J. ENV. L. 315 (2001).

example, we should first address climate change and even various significant but individually low-risk health concerns before worrying that hypothetical computer overlords will oppress us.

Though the full debate about the potential dangers of artificial intelligence is beyond this book's scope, two general observations may help frame the application of that debate to the consideration of autonomous organizations. One is that if artificially intelligent computer systems were an existential risk for us, that would imply (apart from extremely speculative developments, like technological "singularities" toward which autonomous organizations contribute little risk) that computer systems as they are now are already likely an existential risk for us. In other words, if smart software has the opportunity to destroy us, that would be because software already has the ability to destroy us by means of the physical things it can control. Otherwise, newly intelligent software could simply simulate our destruction, not achieve it. While I have no doubt that software can do great harm, I am unaware of any serious argument that – for example – a successful computer hacker could destroy the human race today merely through the skillful use of software. Perhaps if the software that manages nuclear facilities were particularly vulnerable, that would be one avenue of attack, but anything less is probably less than an existential risk. If hacked nuclear weapons (or compromises of similarly dangerous facilities) are a risk, that risk should of course be addressed urgently. If they're not a risk, then it's unclear why the development of artificial intelligence would be a pressing threat.[281] The common law does not ordinarily respond only to speculative, far-off dangers.

To put this observation differently, much as legal personhood for software is probably not a significant danger because it adds little new fundamental legal range for software to a world in which it has one willing human collaborator, if a smart computer program could destroy the world today then that would imply that a very smart human (or a small group of them) would probably have a chance of doing so. If

---

[281] I'm aware, of course, of general arguments that AI will develop slowly by gaining our trust and tricking us, given that with its intellectual superiority, expansive patience, and relatively few physical needs, it could simply bide its time, positioning itself strategically to accomplish its nefarious ends. Again, while interesting in fiction, this sort of speculative concern is far from concrete enough to influence policies in organizational law today.

that is a risk, it should obviously be addressed, but it is not something we ordinarily worry about.

Second, a fear of intelligent algorithms commonly arises today because of their association over the last few years with clumsy and biased statistical aggregation – something that of course can also plague systems without fancy algorithms, neural nets, and so on. For example, in response to the inability to give high-school exams because of COVID-19, the UK made the astonishingly stupid decision in 2020 to make up students' scores by aggregating (1) teachers' predictions of their scores and (2) historical scores in their schools.[282] This was a terrible use of algorithms, egregiously inaccurate and unfair. But the problem is clearly one of educational management; to blame "algorithms" for the disaster is to blame a tool for the people – or human institutions – who have used it poorly. The same is true for racially biased algorithms generally. As much of my legal-academic work has emphasized, I strongly agree that the overreliance on statistical or naive social-scientific classifications is a terrible and common mistake, made appealing only by the faux-sophistication of such tools. But those problems are not a reason to avoid autonomous organizations unless we think that algorithms will necessarily be associated with similar fallacies over the long term. Many intellectual or pseudo-intellectual fads come and go, and it is usually a mistake to regulate or to set legal policy in too short-sighted a way, based on the last scandal or two. That we have poorly rolled out various algorithms to replace human judgment is not an indication that automation itself is problematic, only that it has domain-specific dangers and must be used thoughtfully.

In any event, if robots take over the world, they're unlikely to do it by making contracts or buying houses. Partly this point is just intuitive: evil robots who want to enslave the human race probably don't have much need for breach-of-contract actions or property registers. But perhaps more importantly, as a legal or regulatory matter, the techniques I've proposed earlier in this book make it easier to recognize and normalize software's interactions with the rest of the law; they do not actually enable anything that isn't already available to a malicious actor.

---

[282] See Ben Quinn, *UK Exams Debacle: How Did This Year's Results End Up in Chaos?*, THE GUARDIAN, Aug. 17, 2020, www.theguardian.com/education/2020/aug/17/uk-exams-debacle-how-did-results-end-up-chaos [https://perma.cc/5PQD-6BYP].

Again, just one human being's "personhood" is enough to let software make many contracts or control significant property, as is direct flouting of the law – impersonation of existing legal persons and similar sorts of undetectable fraud. It is implausible that those techniques enable, on their own, a malicious robotic invasion force, and in any event if we are secure against an invasion force only through full consensus – that is, if we're vulnerable if *any* human is willing to empower robots – then we've already lost.

Generally, the broad threats to humanity that my critics are concerned about are similarly speculative and do not arise from the specific legal capabilities of autonomous organizations. For example, Professor LoPucki writes that "[a]n initiator [of an autonomous organization] could program [it] to raise money to finance terrorism or to directly engage in terrorist acts. It could be programmed for genocide or general mayhem."[283] This is true, of course, but again, legal policy is not normally decided in view of that mere possibility. A conventional corporation or trust could be used to "finance terrorism or to directly engage in terrorist acts," and it could be organized "for genocide or general mayhem." That is not an argument against permitting incorporation. When specific abuses are recognized, targeted reforms are usually a sufficient response. Nobody thinks we should look with suspicion on contract law just because there is an occasional contract killing; the solution is to make contract killings illegal and then to enforce that prohibition effectively. Indeed, it may be better if terrorists and other malicious actors use LLCs than if they work entirely outside of the legal system or other opportunities for public view; a similar argument, for example, has been made about anonymity networks like Tor and pseudonymous cryptocurrencies like Bitcoin.[284]

To be clear, I am as opposed to oppression by formalism as anyone; I am not advocating a world in which all decisions are made by formal algorithms or in which there is no opportunity to appeal from the application of mechanical rules to novel or idiosyncratic situations. My goal is simply to open a door to a new, interesting, and potentially

---

[283] LoPucki, *supra* note 24, at 900.
[284] *See, e.g.*, John Bohannan, *Why Criminals Can't Hide Behind Bitcoin*, Sci. N., Mar. 9, 2016, www.sciencemag.org/news/2016/03/why-criminals-cant-hide-behind-bitcoin [https://perma.cc/V5Z9-SFXQ].

productive use of technology. Its use in private, as compared to public, settings seems much more benign because of the "voluntary" nature of the use, the potential for market competition (to permit the technology to expand only to the extent it is useful or desired), and the limited scope of private enterprise. Again, none of this is meant as a utopian argument; I don't speak of "market competition" or "voluntariness" without being critical of those concepts. But such criticism is not sufficient to stop a new kind of legal-transactional technique in its infancy before even determining what its real-world consequences are likely to be.

5.2 PRACTICAL AUTONOMY AND LEGAL FUNCTION

This section considers questions of substantive value directly: Do we have reasons to suppose that permitting autonomous organizations will make the world a better place?

Of course, as background, we don't ordinarily ban transactional techniques just because they are new; we don't ordinarily prevent transactional flexibility just because commentators can speculate about the negative consequences of that flexibility. I have tried to show in this chapter so far that most of the arguments against autonomous organizations are at best ill-formed and speculative, so what we're left with is a novel set of techniques that may seem unusual but are likely at worst neutral – providing a sort of glue or connection between different areas of law that could probably already be achieved less effectively in other ways. Our system doesn't ordinarily treat novelty or unfamiliarity as a basis for outright prohibition.

I don't mean to overstate this point. The most general reason to allow a broad new type of transactional technique is that doing so will increase the value of existing resources by permitting them to be used in ways that their owners desire. That argument is too general because it tends to oppose *all* regulation, and that is not my intent. But ordinarily there has to be a specific reason for banning transactional activity or governance structures – usually some market failure or moral wrong that the regulation would prevent or ameliorate. Here, after sweeping away vague moral arguments framed in terms of dignity and vague instrumental arguments hypothesizing the end of the world from new technologies that haven't even yet been developed, no obvious reason is left.

That train of argumentation is still negative. The positive argument in favor of autonomous organizations, however, is similar. It is essentially the same as the range of creative possibilities suggested in this book's first chapter: autonomous organizations, if desired, achieve goals that allow productive uses of algorithms, whether philanthropic (to commit money to public-serving uses but in a way that is governed by algorithms), administrative (to do the same but for inheritances), commercial (to do the same in order to create demand for investment, purchase, or other action by way of verifiable commitment), or coordinative (to use algorithmic commitments to achieve self-enforcing contracts among groups of parties, within, say, an industry). These are just different ways to organize the motivating examples in Chapter 1.

Autonomous organizations are of course not the only way to achieve these types of goals or to empower algorithms to interact with the rest of the legal system. We could, for example, grant legal personhood by statute in individual cases or enable something short of personhood – maybe a novel type of limited algorithmic company (as Vermont has enacted through its blockchain-based LLCs) or recognition of particular types of freestanding, long-term algorithmic contracts as an alternative to traditional legal organizations. But these alternatives are either too slow (direct regulation by statute) or unnecessarily complicated (why try to architect new types of vehicles for durable, autonomous, enforceable contracts when legal organizations already exist for a similar purpose?).

Similarly and importantly, using autonomous organizations as a placeholder for the activity of autonomous systems provides a convenient locus for liability when the autonomous systems cause harm. The existence of an autonomous organization doesn't prevent negligent or other wrongful developers of an autonomous system from being liable; it simply provides a new, potentially convenient target for liability. As background, it is a common misconception that a "limited liability" entity shields people from the legal consequences of their own torts; organizations like LLCs don't do this, and "I was just following orders" or "I was just doing my job" is not ordinarily a defense to tort liability.[285] For example, it is common to hear stories of a sole proprietor who thinks that setting up an LLC will mean that they won't be liable if they drive a car negligently and thereby cause damage in the course of their business, but this is simply a mistake. Accordingly, autonomous organizations do not *reduce* opportunities for tort liability. They may *expand* those opportunities so long as the autonomous organizations themselves have assets that can be the subject of legal judgments – as compared, for example, to a disorganized operation of an algorithm, not recognized by law, which does not in fact "own" anything and whose assets may be even more difficult to track down. Of course, not all LLCs can pay all their judgments, but that is a general feature of LLCs and is not specific to autonomous organizations; to the extent that feature is socially problematic, the law could address it by requiring LLCs to have insurance (much as automobile drivers are required to have insurance) or by increasing the registration fees or taxes on LLCs.

There is a further possibility that shouldn't be squelched before it has a chance to prove itself: autonomous organizations as a means for engaging in commerce directly and in perhaps more efficient a manner than traditional for-profit companies. A network of vending machines or a cloud-storage broker may not *need* a human or organizational owner; it may be able to offer items at lower prices if it needn't produce a profit, and it is at least a possibility that the dictates of an algorithm will make a service more competitive, at least in some contexts, than the passions of a business-school graduate or the forces of the private or public equity markets. Moreover, the notion of this sort of business is

---

[285] *See* BAYERN, *supra* note 72, at 80–81 for legal background on this point. Working for an organization can be a legal defense to tort liability in limited situations, like when the work is done for the federal government or for a nonprofit organization. *See* 28 U.S.C. § 2679 (b)(1) ("The remedy against the United States ... for injury or loss of property, or personal injury or death arising or resulting from the negligent or wrongful act or omission of any employee of the Government while acting within the scope of his office or employment is exclusive of any other civil action or proceeding for money damages by reason of the same subject matter against the employee whose act or omission gave rise to the claim or against the estate of such employee."); 42 U.S.C. § 14503(a) ("[Under certain conditions], no volunteer of a nonprofit organization or governmental entity shall be liable for harm caused by an act or omission of the volunteer on behalf of the organization or entity ....").

not in fact unfamiliar; we might conceive an autonomous business simply as a conventional not-for-profit organization that requires minimal manual oversight. The market in corporate ownership has proven useful in contexts where new owners may be able to unlock efficiencies that prior owners were unable or unwilling to unlock; that is, allowing a company to be acquired may be a straightforward mechanism to achieve allocational efficiency – the transition of ownership over legal assets toward those who value them most highly, which in a commercial context will normally match those who can unlock the most value from them. Thus, for example, the sale of a company may create strategic opportunities that wouldn't exist without the sale. But for businesses where no such value is likely to arise – or perhaps in businesses where the original owners do not want it to arise, because they have some goal other than maximal economic growth (such as environmental concerns or an interest in the wellbeing of local constituencies) – eliminating the market for ownership by providing for the algorithmic disposition of the business does no harm, simply because there is no need for the potential for allocative efficiency that the market for control unlocks.[286] And the potential economic benefit, again, is that there is no need for such an organization to produce profits for private shareholders. That profit, broadly speaking, is a sort of fee that customers pay for the putative efficiencies engendered by a market for corporate control; if that market doesn't have a reason to exist in particular contexts, there is no need for customers to pay the fee.[287]

Permitting the formal type of autonomous organization that I have described will avoid requiring the law to specify, in advance, a standard

---

[286] See ROBERT COOTER & THOMAS ULEN, LAW & ECONOMICS 135–38 (6th ed. 2012).

[287] Thus, for example, credit unions appear to be as efficient for customers as banks, if not more so, as judged by borrowing and savings rates. Credit unions are similar to banks except that they have no private shareholders. Mutual insurance operates on a similar model, as does Vanguard. In all those cases, a market for control with a group of shareholders providing potential oversight is not needed because of relatively stable groups of customers that can provide the equivalent form of oversight: in some sense the "shareholders" of a credit union are simply the members who benefit from the organization's operation, and the "shareholders" of a mutual insurance company are the insureds. That is simply another way of saying that there is no separate group of third-party shareholders who profit at the expense of the customers. For that reason, the model of self-ownership is conceptually superior for customers as long as competition in the market for corporate control would not have generated efficiencies in their favor that would exceed the loss to them from "fees" to third-party shareholders.

of autonomy, intelligence, or any other characteristic that is necessary or sufficient for legal "rights." Even the best philosophers have struggled with the definition of humanity and its implication for human rights, leading to polarizing results.[288] There is clearly currently no social consensus on the question,[289] and such a consensus is particularly unlikely to emerge *before* intelligent autonomous systems become more important. The law generally trails the development of new technologies, offering inflexible responses when flexible ones would be more suitable; autonomous organizations are one area in which the flexibility of the existing structures happens to suit the open-ended nature of future technological development.

---

[288] *E.g.*, PETER SINGER, PRACTICAL ETHICS 182–90 (2d ed. 1993) (arguing for a limited conception of rights for severely disabled humans).

[289] *Cf.* Solum, *supra* note 132.

6 THE LIMITATIONS AND LEGAL IMPLICATIONS OF AUTONOMOUS ORGANIZATIONS

Common law, and indeed much of the rest of the law, is not centrally coordinated. Even when law is statutory, there is usually no systematic effort in common-law jurisdictions to identify how changes in one area of law put pressure on other areas. Even within a single legal subject, changes to one doctrine often have effects that courts and commentators don't notice or quickly accommodate. For example, as a technical legal example, it is not widely enough recognized that the more widely and flexibly a jurisdiction applies cover damages for breach of contract (i.e., damages to pay for substitute performance), the less reason it has to use specific performance as a remedy.[290] But the same pattern applies much more broadly: a change to a doctrine in tort law can weaken or strengthen the justifications for a doctrine in property law, and it often takes a long time in a common-law jurisdiction, which normally operates without comprehensive initiatives to harmonize the law, to recognize and accommodate the connection between the two doctrines.

The story of organizational law – corporations, partnerships, LLCs, and so forth – in the United States has largely been the story of increases in the flexibility of arrangements for internal governance. Early

---

[290] *See* Melvin A. Eisenberg, *Actual and Virtual Specific Performance, the Theory of Efficient Breach, and the Indifference Principle in Contract Law*, 93 CAL. L. REV. 975, 1041–49 (2005). In that article, Professor Eisenberg analyzes cover damages – that is, damages equal to the cost of a substitute performance – as a "virtual" sort of specific performance, compared to "actual" specific performance. The proper result is a sort of hydraulic interchange between cover and specific performance: to the extent a jurisdiction applies the concept of cover broadly, it can and probably should reduce the availability of specific performance, and vice versa.

corporations were chartered by specific legislation to accomplish narrow purposes, like building a bridge or engaging in particular shipping operations;[291] later, general-purpose corporations, usually with the scope to engage in "any lawful business," came to dominate US business law;[292] eventually, the mandatory structures for the internal governance of corporations loosened considerably, so that mechanisms like voting trusts and eventually custom shareholder agreements became enforceable;[293] and finally came extremely flexible LLCs, starting in the late 1970s and solidifying their influence in the last few decades. This story is perhaps a simple demonstration of public-choice theory, which would explain the increased flexibility that the law provides for the internal structure of organizations as a result of interest-group politics: there are concentrated interests (like the managers of organizations) in favor of greater internal organizational flexibility, and there are no powerful interests specifically opposed to such flexibility, so as a result there is a reason for legislatures to increase the flexibility of corporations and to adopt new organizational forms like LLCs.[294] This increased flexibility, in turn, yields transactional generativity – of the sort I have tried to demonstrate in, for example, Chapters 2 through 4 of this book.

That generativity has consequences: it enables private parties to achieve their goals through legally enforceable operating agreements, contracts, and other instruments. These consequences in turn put pressure on other areas of law. Doctrines in property law, contract, law, tort law, and other legal subjects have not been designed with the possibility of autonomous organizations in mind, just as they were not designed to accommodate many other transactional organizational structures (and other changes) that have developed over time. A conservative impulse is perhaps to squash that sort of generativity,

---

[291] *See supra* notes 85–95 and accompanying text. For more historical background on early corporate law in the United States, see Samuel Williston, *History of the Law of Business Corporations before 1800*, 2 HARV. L. REV. 105 (1888).

[292] *See* HERBERT HOVENKAMP, ENTERPRISE AND AMERICAN LAW 1836–1937 (1991); John Dewey, *The Historic Background of Corporate Legal Personality*, 35 YALE L.J. 655, 662–67 (1926).

[293] *See, e.g.,* MBCA § 7.32 for an example of modern flexibility in the internal governance of closely held corporations.

[294] For background, see, for example, MANCUR OLSON, THE LOGIC OF COLLECTIVE ACTION: PUBLIC GOODS AND THE THEORY OF GROUPS (rev. ed. 1971); *cf.* BAYERN, *supra* note 72, at 183–84.

as the previous chapter argued against, but a different response is simply to accommodate it: as one area of the law changes, others must keep pace or else they will become increasingly out of date. Because it is not possible to stop autonomous organizations completely, and because the only way to prevent the need for one area of law to adapt to changes in other areas would be to stifle all legal change (a prospect that all but ultraconservative commentators would reject), it is important to work through the implications of autonomous organizations for other areas of law.[295]

This chapter covers several potentially important adaptations that the law might make in response to autonomous organizations and the increased flexibility in organizational law underlying them. My goal, however, is not to predict the future; other adaptations may well be necessary. The hope is that discussion here lays the groundwork for considering several of the problems posed by autonomous organizations and for developing solutions to those problems. In engaging in such a discussion, the chapter also draws attention to some limitations and pitfalls of autonomous organizations.

6.1 THE ROLE OF INTENT IN THE PRIVATE LAW

In a world in which the law permits algorithms to have direct, binding legal effects, it makes little sense for legal doctrines to pay much attention to the "intent" of the algorithm. But many legal doctrines do care about the intent and other mental states of the wrongdoer or the victim. They probably shouldn't – at least not as much as they traditionally have done. Autonomous organizations serve as an impetus to continue a helpful trend in the law away from relying on intent as a predicate of civil liability.

To put it differently, there are good reasons for the law to care considerably less about intent than it currently does anyway, apart from autonomous organizations. Predicating liability on intent has unnecessarily complicated the private law and in some areas has made it very

---

[295] *Cf.* Lon L. Fuller, *The Forms and Limits of Adjudication*, 92 HARV. L. REV. 353, 394–404 (discussing "polycentric" problems).

difficult for wronged victims to recover damages, both in general and particularly from groups and organizations. To be clear, my argument is not that the law should ignore intent entirely; it is simply that some intent-related distinctions that the law currently draws can be collapsed and that intent should rarely be a necessary condition for liability. In cases where a bad intent is found, it can and should lead to criminal liability, punitive damages, presumptions against the wrongdoer, and other legal sanctions – but the elements of private causes of action should not ordinarily include the intent of the wrongdoer.

6.1.1 Intentional Torts, Conventional Organizations, and Autonomous Organizations

The claim that the law should deemphasize intent (and particularly the claim that it should not be essential for civil liability) may initially seem extreme because there is a large collection of what are commonly referred to as "intentional torts"; indeed, the American Law Institute is currently working on a project to restate the law of "Intentional Torts to Persons" as part of the *Restatement (Third) of Torts*. But there has long been a recognition among at least some leading torts scholars that the "intent" in many or most intentional torts is more a distraction than an analytically helpful element. As Professor Steve Sugarman put it in 2002, speaking of the tort of battery, which is the label tort law uses for wrongful intentional contact with other human beings:

> I reject the idea that we benefit from having a separate tort for uncon-sented-to, offensive, physical touching. Rather, I believe we should ask whether the touching of one by another was reasonable or not. If it was reasonable, then generally there should be no liability, and certainly not fault-based liability. On the other hand, if the conduct was unreason-able, then the defendant should normally be liable . . . .[296]

In other words, as Professor Sugarman describes in more recent work, "both negligence law and battery rest on a common fault principle";[297] liability largely depends, and should depend, on whether the

---

[296] Stephen D. Sugarman, *Rethinking Tort Doctrine: Visions of a Restatement (Fourth) of Torts*, 50 UCLA L. REV. 585, 594–95 (2002).
[297] Stephen D. Sugarman, *Restating the Tort of Battery*, 10 J. TORT L. 197, 198 (2018).

wrongdoer was at fault – that is, whether they acted unreasonably or wrongfully – not on their intent. The separation of intentional torts from the broader tort of negligence (liability for unreasonably causing physical harm) has led to unnecessary doctrinal complication. For example, even if one intentionally touches another, there is no liability if the touching was consensual, but the doctrine of "consent" has been constructed artificially so that it serves to eliminate tort liability so long as people act reasonably. As Professor Sugarman has described it:

> [I]f one brushes against another while moving down the aisle of a crowded bus, or if one gently taps a stranger on the shoulder to ask the time, and we think these defendants should not be liable for their conduct, then the reason is that such behavior – unlike spitting on another's shoe in contempt, for example – is reasonable ... . Similarly, when battery doctrine now allows a defense of self-defense, it is basically saying that when self-defense is properly exercised, the actor, who has inflicted harm, has acted reasonably. My vision ... would express this directly, without requiring the complexities of a prima facie case plus a defense.[298]

To be clear, in Sugarman's example, people out in public don't actually "consent" to being touched, but the law may regard their consent as "implied." As Sugarman is suggesting, it would be much simpler not to require a defense of consent in the first place by treating the putative wrongdoer's conduct as rightful if it is objectively reasonable and wrongful if it is not. Classifying the conduct that way can be done without regard to the putative wrongdoer's intent.

So far, all that is at stake is the terminology or conceptual organization of tort law.[299] But proving intent often is the main or only way for victims to recover for certain kinds of harm – particularly, for emotional and economic harms. That is, in US tort law in general, there is said to be "no duty" to prevent negligent injuries to others as long as those injuries are "purely" emotional or economic.[300] If a manager,

---

[298] Sugarman, *supra* note 296, at 595.

[299] In the two articles just mentioned, *supra* notes 296 and 297, Professor Sugarman describes several types of cases in which tort law's concern with intent might reach the wrong results even in simple cases of physical harm by and to individuals.

[300] The law distinguishes "purely" emotional and economic harms from those that are a consequence of a physical injury. Thus, the pain of a broken bone from a car accident is recoverable in negligence (that is, even without the intent of the person who wrongfully

acquaintance, or stranger treats another human being in such a way that the victim feels abused or deeply insulted, that is not normally a legal wrong even if the abuser has acted objectively unreasonably. There are, instead, pockets of particular types of liability that depend on intent, like the tort of "intentional infliction of emotional distress," which ordinarily imposes liability only if the wrongdoer "intentionally or recklessly" causes severe emotional distress in a way that is "extreme and outrageous."[301] A similar pattern applies to "purely" economic harms: negligently giving incorrect information to an unrelated third party doesn't normally lead to liability; liability applies only under certain conditions – such as if there is "fraud," and (as described by the *Restatement (Second) of Torts*) fraud normally requires that the person supplying information

(a) knows or believes that the matter is not as he represents it to be,
(b) does not have the confidence in the accuracy of his representation that he states or implies, or
(c) knows that he does not have the basis for his representation that he states or implies.[302]

This state of affairs points up what seems, in retrospect, like an obvious hole in the law: organizations can take significant actions even though they lack an "intent" that is localized to particular humans within the organization and therefore recognizable to the law. For example, an

---

caused the injury), but the pain of being shouted at by an abusive manager is not. Similarly, a negligent driver of a car that crashes into a shop is liable for the physical damage that the crash causes, but a negligent driver who crashes a car on a bridge, shutting down the bridge for several days and thereby causing a shop at the foot of the bridge to lose revenue, is not liable to the shop for their negligence.

[301] *See* RESTATEMENT (SECOND) OF TORTS § 46 (1965). The tort is called "outrage" in some states, and the phrase "extreme and outrageous" is something of an ill-defined term of art. The comment to the *Restatement (Second) of Torts* tries helpfully to define it in a way that ends up being unintentionally amusing: "Generally," it says, that element of the tort is satisfied if "the recitation of the facts to an average member of the community would arouse his resentment against the actor, and lead him to exclaim, 'Outrageous!'" *Id.* cmt. d. It may be helpful to observe that the word "outrageous" has not historically meant what many people assume it means; the word does not derive from "rage" but from a form of the French *outré*, which comes from the Latin *ultra*. In other words, the word simply means *ultra*-age – that is, something that is *ultra*, or beyond the bounds of, decent conduct. *See* OXFORD ENGLISH DICTIONARY, "outrage, n.", OED Online, Oxford University Press, May 2021, www.oed.com/view/Entry/133856.

[302] RESTATEMENT (SECOND) OF TORTS § 526.

organization might act in a way that looks a lot like fraud – benefiting from false information it gives to third parties – even no human in the organization has the intent or knowledge that fraud requires. The organization can escape liability as a result.

The problem is of course magnified to the extent autonomous organizations begin to operate, because an autonomous organization, at least as powered by today's technologies, probably never has an intent. This point is more complicated than it may appear, however, for at least three separate reasons.

First, an autonomous organization may well be *part of* an intent – for example, the intent of the people who have set it in motion, or of those who somehow take control or influence it to achieve fraudulent goals – even if it lacks intent itself. This possibility seems to pose little problem for the law: if a bad actor uses an autonomous organization as an instrumentality to achieve some legal wrong, the law can still identify and remedy the wrong. The autonomous organization does not appear to get in the way of meaningful enforcement as a conceptual matter; of course, using LLCs to shield activity may lead to practical problems for plaintiffs or law-enforcement officials, but that is not a problem particular to autonomous organizations. For example, if someone sets up an autonomous organization and then invites people to contribute to it on false pretenses, the law can already address that wrong, and it should have little difficulty using tools like "veil piercing" and turnover orders to make sure that the wrongdoer (1) is liable and (2) pays a judgment with funds to which they have access. In general, law has little difficulty in responding to broad patterns of activity that a wrongful actor has set in motion; occasionally the law stumbles by narrowing its focus too much (for example, in treating harms as indirect and therefore outside the original actor's scope of liability, or in restricting its focus to a particular action rather than a sequence of actions), but it will not require significant changes in legal doctrine for the law to pay more attention to long-term technological activity that can be started by the press of a button.[303]

---

[303] As a related example, today, negligence law can easily address a bad decision made by a driver while driving, but it has more difficulty addressing the reasonableness of a driver's decision to drive in the first place. That sort of decision is not beyond the law's reach; a decision to drive in the middle of a dangerous snowstorm, fire, or riot could be evaluated

Second, briefly, artificially intelligent systems might one day progress to the point where we recognize in them an intent, along with other mental states or characteristics currently reserved for humans (or at least humans and animals, depending on the particular mental state or characteristic). This is not a problem, though; it just means that the underlying concern about intent could eventually resolve itself through advancement in artificial intelligence.

Third, both more importantly and more subtly, while autonomous organizations lack literal intent in a way that the law can currently recognize – nobody thinks a computer system of today's technology has its own independent motivations – it *can* have "knowledge," and often knowledge is enough to categorize activity as "intentional" even if the activity is not literally intentional. In other words, in law, "intentional" is often a legal term of art that means "intentional or knowing" or "intentional or reckless," as some of the definitions quoted and discussed above suggest. (Although the law's treatment of recklessness is complicated, one simple definition of the concept amounts to "knowingly acting negligently," so a system that possesses knowledge can probably act recklessly even if it lacks the capacity to intend to cause harm.)

It is easy enough to see how software can have knowledge: it has access to storage and memory that can record facts, and that knowledge can be inspected. Moreover, the law sometimes deems organizations to have knowledge because they have received particular notifications or because knowledge of their agents is imputed to them.[304] That type of

---

in a negligence cause of action. But a decision to drive more than is necessary, or for frivolous purposes, is not something that the common law tends to address. For the germinal theoretical analysis of this sort of concern and legal responses to it, see Steven Shavell, *Strict Liability Versus Negligence*, 9 J. LEGAL STUD. 1 (1980) (raising the problem of "activity levels" – e.g., *how much* driving is efficient – in tort law). This problem may in fact become easier to analyze as driving becomes more automated; once it is widely recognized that self-driving cars are safer than human drivers, it may well become easier for courts to recognize a driver's decision to drive in the first place as negligent.

[304] *See, e.g.*, RESTATEMENT (THIRD) OF AGENCY § 5.01(1) ("A notification is a manifestation that is made in the form required by agreement among parties or by applicable law, or in a reasonable manner in the absence of an agreement or an applicable law, with the intention of affecting the legal rights and duties of the notifier in relation to rights and duties of persons to whom the notification is given."); *id.* § 5.02 ("[N]otice of a fact that an agent knows or has reason to know is imputed to the principal if knowledge of the fact is material to the agent's duties to the principal . . . .").

knowledge is relatively straightforward, and it means that even an auton-omous organization can "knowingly" take action as far as the law is concerned – and that it could thereby commit at least some intentional torts. When knowledge arises from notifications (which can be verified relatively easy) or knowledge of human agents (which is at least a conventional question for which the law has conventional techniques to detect truth), it poses no special problems. Knowledge that potentially arises from the working memory of a software system is not practically problematic; the inspection of the working memory of conventional (as opposed, perhaps, to quantum) algorithms is at least conceptually straightforward, regardless of the particular physical form the memory takes or the technology with which it is implemented.

Not all knowledge is so simple, however. At any point, a computer program's current processing may lead it to a state that cannot be reached unless some precondition is true, even if that precondition is not stored explicitly by the computer program.[305] The program can rely on the fact that the precondition is true, and it may be said to "know" it just as much as it knows what is explicitly in its working memory. As a simple example, a program can "know" that a particular user is a customer even if it has not retained knowledge of that custo-mer's identity, as long as the software is securely written in such a way that only customers may access the relevant part of the program. In this way, software can act as if various assumptions are true even if it does not keep those assumptions "in mind," just as humans can act with tacit, unconscious, or unexpressed knowledge of the world.[306] This

---

[305] To demonstrate this in more technical terms using pseudocode, consider software such as

```
if (A) then do B * followed by C;
```

This code tests whether a condition A is true and then executes B and C, which could be any algorithms. At the point in the code indicated by the asterisk, the program can be said to "know" that A is (or was once) true, at least given some technical assumptions not worth elaborating here, but the fact that A was once true is never stored explicitly in the program. B may take a while to execute and the conditions that made A true may change, but even so, when C executes it can do so with the "knowledge" that A was once true even though that fact does not appear in the computer's memory. Indeed, this remains true even if the code is overwritten as the program runs, so that there would be no record at all of how the program got into its then-current state.

[306] *Cf.* LON FULLER, MELVIN ARON EISENBERG, & MARK P. GERGEN, BASIC CONTRACT LAW 858–59, 901–02 (9th ed. 2013) (describing tacit assumptions – in humans, of course – in the context of contract law).

type of knowledge may be much harder for courts or other legal actors to verify, because reverse-engineering the state of an algorithm is both practically and theoretically a much more difficult program than inspecting software's working memory. In the general case, the problem is probably not computable, much as one computer program cannot in the general case analyze whether another computer program will terminate of its own accord.[307]

In short, then, (1) today's software doesn't have literal intent; (2) it may have knowledge, which is sometimes sufficient to qualify as "intent" under legal tests; (3) some of the knowledge of software may be relatively easily analyzed; (4) but some of it is exceedingly complex and perhaps noncomputable, and therefore not necessarily verifiable to courts or determinable by the legal system. These facts imply that, in at least some cases, the intent of autonomous organizations may elude the legal system. That conclusion shouldn't be difficult to imagine. For example, suppose an autonomous cloud-storage system or news-aggregation service has, through its algorithmic processing, made many statements that would clearly qualify as false and objectively unreasonable, and suppose third parties have relied on these misstatements and suffered losses as a result. The losses arise without conventional "fraud" if the intent of the autonomous system cannot be proven, and it is easy to picture cases where it could not be proven: for example, analysis of the code suggests the problem results from an error, or from the complex optimization of various factors in ways that are difficult to analyze – or even from an optimization that is clearly in what we might regard as the "interest" (at least as we might analyze interests in human terms) of the autonomous organization that the software manages.

It would be extremely problematic if, in such cases, an autonomous organization escapes liability merely because it lacks an intent. This may, consistent with the form of intuitively appealing arguments against autonomous organizations that I critiqued in Chapter 5, suggest to some that autonomous organizations should not be permitted to function. But this would stifle too much. Given that autonomous

---

[307] *See* A.M. Turing, *On Computable Numbers, with an Application to the Entscheidungsproblem* ("Decision Problem"), 42 Proc. London Math. Soc. 230 (1937); for a general modern introduction, see https://en.wikipedia.org/wiki/Halting_problem.

organizations are probably very difficult to prevent anyway (as discussed in Chapter 4), and also given that there are relatively simple solutions to the problem of irremediable fraud by autonomous organizations, the solution should probably be more narrowly tailored.[308] In particular, courts should begin to recognize situations that are akin to fraud even where intent is missing. Contract and tort doctrines already provide remedies for non-fraudulent misrepresentation,[309] and an appropriate response to the lack of intent of autonomous (and other) organizations should be for the law to begin to collapse distinctions between misrepresentations in general and fraudulent (i.e., intentional) misrepresentations in particular.

I suspect this sort of change will happen naturally as courts begin to see harms caused by complex systems for which intent is not easy to prove. It is not a radical change to the law; it does not throw off other doctrines, is not hard to implement, and does not threaten to open the floodgates of liability. It is a straightforward, incremental development in common law. It requires only that courts notice a situation that deserves a remedy and relax the requirements associated with knowledge or intent in the causes of action that would achieve the remedy.[310]

This sort of suggestion does not need to wait for the rise of autonomous organizations; it is likely to arise anyway even without them. For example, complex but conventional and familiar algorithms on the website of an online vendor might "accidentally defraud" customers by

---

[308] Moreover, the argument that the possibility of their escaping liability for fraud should lead the law to prohibit autonomous organizations proves too much, because it suggests that conventional organizations be prohibited and disbanded as well.

[309] *See, e.g.*, Restatement (Second) of Contracts § 496; Restatement (Second) of Torts §§ 552 et seq.

[310] For a general effort to harmonize the legal treatment of artificial intelligence and humans, see Ryan Abbott, The Reasonable Robot: Artificial Intelligence and the Law (2020). For the specific kind of problem I am aiming to address in the text, simply relaxing the requirements of intent or knowledge is simpler and probably a more adaptive response than generally trying to compare an algorithm to a hypothetical human in a similar position, as has been proposed for (e.g.) self-driving cars. *See, e.g., id.* at 70.

Other changes to tort law, through the normal long-term processes of common law, are possible too. For example, to the extent it becomes difficult to analyze the reasonableness of potential injurers, tort law could come to care more about the reasonable expectations of consumers, imposing a sort of strict liability whenever those reasonable expectations are violated. This would amount to a revival and broadening of the "consumer expectations" test for defective products that is used in some states but which was not adopted in the American Law Institute's Restatement (Third) of Torts: Products Liability.

displaying incorrect information. Again, doctrines of non-fraudulent mis-representation may be a sufficient response, but to the extent a legal remedy depends on proving "knowledge," it will probably be better to relax that requirement even in cases where the harm has resulted from a conventional organization that uses software, much less an autonomous one.

As a potential victim of fraud rather than a potential wrongdoer, autonomous organizations are probably already on solid enough legal footing. Fraud requires reliance on a misrepresentation, but "reliance" ordinarily is taken just to require causation, not any particular mental state. It should be easy enough to prove that a material misrepresentation caused software (and thus an autonomous organization) to change its behavior.

6.1.2 Intent and Contracts

Contract law is ordinarily described as proceeding based on an objective theory of interpretation; that is, we don't care about a "meeting of the minds," and communications are said to have the meaning they would have to reasonable recipients. Such a view is a bit of an over-simplification; while modern contract law does use an objective theory of interpretation, there is a complex interplay between subjective meanings that the parties adopt and the "reasonable" meanings of their words to others. For example, though a "meeting of the minds" is not required for a contract, if a meeting of the minds does occur – that is, if parties subjectively reach an agreement with each other – then under general modern US contract principles that agreement will govern even if the parties have reached the agreement using words that would reasonably have a different meaning to others.[311]

None of this poses a significant problem for autonomous organizations that are meant to enter contracts. The words issued by an autonomous organization will simply have the meaning that others reasonably understand them to have. The possibility of a subjective agreement would simply not arise.

---

[311] This is at least the view of the RESTATEMENT (SECOND) OF CONTRACTS in § 201(1) ("Where the parties have attached the same meaning to a promise or agreement or a term thereof, it is interpreted in accordance with that meaning.").

At the edges, autonomous organizations might put some pressure on particular, narrow doctrines of contract law. For example, a rule of contract law holds that an offeree cannot accept an offer of a unilateral contract – that is, an offer accepted by taking an action, as opposed to making a promise – without knowledge of the offer. If the knowledge of an autonomous organization is difficult to discern, it should not be difficult for courts to interpret this requirement, when the contract is purportedly accepted by an autonomous organization, by replacing the requirement of knowledge with one that the software that controls the autonomous organization have received or processed the offer as input in some way. (The doctrine does not, and should not, require that the offer be a but-for cause of the action that constitutes acceptance.) Precisely how courts might stretch this doctrine – or related ones, like the *Peerless*[312] doctrine, that depend on the parties' subjective intent or understanding – is less important than that they not apply it formalistically to new types of organizations.[313]

The doctrines of mistake in contract law may interact with autonomous organizations in interesting ways. If a vending machine that sells snacks malfunctions, the seller may lose a few hundred dollars, but if the vending machines are controlled by a centralized artificial intelligence that introduces errors on a large scale, the seller may suffer significantly greater losses. Existing doctrines concerning problems like typographical errors, such as the contract doctrine of unilateral mistake, have not been significantly tested in cases where two software systems conclude a contract together, and it is unclear how courts will respond to that problem. The closest we have come to that situation on a large scale is probably the "flash crash" of 2010,[314] in which simple

---

[312] Raffles v. Wichelhaus, 159 Eng. Rep. 375 (1864).

[313] In the law of offer and acceptance, some other doctrines advert to the offeree's knowledge, but these will likely be less relevant to autonomous organizations. To put it differently, autonomous organizations need not avail themselves of these doctrines in order to function successfully in contract law. For example, silence may constitute acceptance in limited circumstances if the offeree stays silent with an intent to accept the offer. *See* RESTATEMENT (SECOND) OF CONTRACTS § 69(1)(b) (silence operates as acceptance when "the offeror has stated or given the offeree reason to understand that assent may be manifested by silence or inaction, and the offeree in remaining silent and inactive intends to accept the offer").

[314] See Graham Bowley, *The Flash Crash, in Miniature*, N.Y. TIMES, Nov. 9, 2010, at B1.

technical mistakes compounded to cause the US stock market to lose about 10 percent of its value temporarily for no substantive economic reason. Authorities appear to have been largely successful in "canceling" trades caused by that series of technical errors,[315] but it may be more difficult to do so in a more distributed context, or with errors that arise more slowly and on which more innocent parties rely.

That said, the doctrine governing typographical errors has a relatively straightforward, adaptive application to autonomous organizations: the general rule is simply that mistakes that the other party knew about or should have known about (given, for example, their extreme departure from a typical price) are not the basis of a binding contract. If the autonomous organization takes advantage of a mistake in (say) a price posted by another party, it should be easy enough for the law to process the situation under the traditional rule that parties that *should* have known about the mistake can't take advantage of it. That is, the mistake may be judged largely in the abstract, based on hypothetical parties, rather than on the mental states of actual parties.

To put it differently, to the extent that knowledge matters and that it is difficult to prove that software actually knew about a mistake in a way a human might have known, contract law may favor autonomous organizations unfairly. To address this problem, courts can simply expand their interpretation of what errors the autonomous organization should have been aware of; the more errors included in that category, the less opportunity the autonomous organization will have to take advantage of others' typographical mistakes.[316]

6.1.3 Punishing Bad Intent

Much of the law, especially the criminal law, aims to punish the bad intent of legal actors as a way to deter that intent and also to exact

---

[315] *See id.*

[316] There is a range of possibilities for the law's future adaptation to autonomous organizations, depending on the form they take and the policy considerations that courts come to find important. For example, perhaps courts will decide that AIs are not capable of legally recognized mistakes – that they should be treated, for the purposes of contract law, as if they intend everything they do. That would be a policy choice; nothing in existing doctrine or in legal policy necessarily dictates it. But it is one of the plausible choices common-law courts could make.

retribution. Today's software probably lacks any capacity for suffering, so retribution is off the table, but clearly software does not lack the ability to be deterred; software can process legal sanctions as costs just as humans do. Moreover, interestingly, it is not clear that today's software lacks an ability to experience something like an ethical conflict, depending on how it is designed to evaluate its "interests"; thus, as for some humans, legal sanctions may make decisions very "difficult" for some programs or autonomous organizations, even if only by complicating their decision-making.[317]

6.2 DRIFT, ABUSE, AND FORMALISM IN ORGANIZATIONAL LAW

The hijacking of corporate machinery for personal ends, and the degree to which such corporate machinery is treated formalistically, are themes throughout conventional organizational law. Indeed, the themes of advantage-taking and formalism run through most of the law. Autonomous organizations may raise, however, a few special problems of formalism, the drift over time between circumstances and legal instruments, and the abuse of organizational processes.

For the purposes of this discussion, autonomous organizations have a few relevant characteristics; these characteristics are not unique to autonomous organizations, but they may be especially important in considering the problems that autonomous organizations may run into. First, they have indefinite duration and potentially last forever; as the LLC statutes put it, LLCs by default have "perpetual duration."[318] Second, at least given today's technology – software that might run a simple organization but have difficulty responding to broader circumstantial changes in law and facts – they face a risk that an original operating agreement may fail to predict future circumstances. For one

---

[317] *See* Drew McDermott, *Why Ethics Is a High Hurdle for AI*, North American Conference on Computers and Philosophy (NA-CAP), July 2008, https://web.archive.org/web/20190731201113/http://www.cs.yale.edu/homes/dvm/papers/ethical-machine.pdf (referring to an artificially intelligent program that possibly "knew what an ethical conflict was like" even if it was not "ever *in* a real ethical bind").

[318] *E.g.*, RULLCA § 108(c).

thing, the world may simply drift from the expectations of those who originally set the autonomous organization in motion; experience has shown that it is difficult to fashion legal rules that accommodate all changing social practices, policies, and technologies.[319] For another, experience with cybersecurity has demonstrated that it is impossible to prevent hacking and other computer misuse in all its forms, and as a result, an operating agreement that causes the decisions of software to manage an organization may be subject to unpredicted malicious actors. This possibility will still obtain, of course, even if the operating agreement tries to anticipate some amount of hacking and guard against its risk with legal provisions; that is just an alternative attempt at a defense against hacking, and, just like software, it is subject to unpredicted use and abuse. Chapter 2's discussion of the general isomorphism between software and legal agreements is relevant here, in that agreements can be "hacked" in much the same way as software: by malicious actors taking advantages that work formally even though they weren't intended by the original design.[320] Indeed, the difference between legitimate and illegitimate uses of both legal agreements and software is often the subject of deep dispute; there is no obvious way to distinguish one from the other in the general case.

This poses a problem for autonomous organizations, although as just suggested it is not a unique problem: the problem arises every time there is a legal agreement, and it is magnified every time an agreement is expected to govern the long-term affairs of an organization. The more that autonomous organizations are used, the more that courts will need to grapple with the proper ways to intervene in the long-term govern-ance of LLC operating agreements.

It is worth pointing out again that autonomous organizations needn't have a single form; an operating agreement may, for example,

---

[319] *Compare, e.g.*, Baltimore & Ohio R.R. Co. v. Goodman, 275 U.S. 66 (1927) (laying out a specific rule to govern the conduct of automobile drivers) *with* Pokora v. Wabash Railway Co., 292 U.S. 98 (1934) (demonstrating that the prior fact-specific rule couldn't last even ten years and observing that "[s]tandards of prudent conduct are declared at times by courts, but they are taken over from the facts of life").

[320] *See* Juliet P. Kostritsky, *Plain Meaning vs. Broad Interpretation: How the Risk of Opportunism Defeats a Unitary Default Rule For Interpretation*, 96 Ky. L.J. 43, 90 (2007) (discussing opportunistic "chiseling" at contract terms and its implication for the proper interpretive regime for contract law).

recognize the decisions of an algorithm that is partly implemented by humans, and human groups can be corrupted just as software can; which is riskier is just an empirical question. Moreover, the algorithms to which an operating agreement defers needn't be conventional. They can be distributed, like blockchains, but also can involve mutually independent, reinforcing components that act as checks and balances on one another, just as a public constitution may try to prevent political abuses by allocating powers to different parts of potential future governments.

There are three particular strands of jurisprudence in organizational law that courts and legislatures may find useful to prevent the drift and abuse of autonomous organizations. The rest of this section considers those three strands in turn.

6.2.1 Legal Recognition of Evolving Expectations

In implementing the rights and duties within closely held organizations, courts have developed a doctrine that permits the reasonable expectations of shareholders to govern the organization even if those expectations depart from the formal text and structures of the operating agreement (or its corporate equivalent, the articles of incorporation and bylaws). As one well-known court case put it:

> Professor [F. Hodge O'Neal], perhaps the foremost authority on close corporations, points out that many close corporations are companies based on personal relationships that give rise to certain "reasonable expectations" on the part of those acquiring an interest in the close corporation. Those "reasonable expectations" include, for example, the parties' expectation that they will participate in the management of the business or be employed by the company . . . .
>
> Thus, when personal relations among the participants in a close corporation break down, the "reasonable expectations" the participants had, for example, an expectation that their employment would be secure, or that they would enjoy meaningful participation in the management of the business – become difficult if not impossible to fulfill. In other words, when the personal relationships among the participants break down, the majority shareholder, because of his greater voting power, is in a position to terminate

the minority shareholder's employment and to exclude him from participation in management decisions.

Some may argue that the minority shareholder should have bargained for greater protection before agreeing to accept his minority shareholder position in a close corporation. However, the practical realities of this particular business situation oftentimes do not allow for such negotiations.[321]

As the modern version of Professor O'Neal's treatise puts it, "One of the most significant trends in the law of close corporations in recent years is the increasing willingness of courts to look to the reasonable expectations of shareholders to determine whether 'oppression' or similar grounds exist as a justification for involuntary dissolution or another remedy."[322] Moreover, these reasonable expectations may change over time, particularly in long-running organizations.[323]

Of course, this doctrine does not apply precisely to autonomous organization; it is a doctrine that benefits shareholders. Still, the existence and development of this doctrine can make it easier for courts to recognize that in the fact-intensive context of organizational operations, the text of an operating agreement is not sacrosanct; instead, organizations serve functional ends, and courts can pay attention to what those involved in the organization reasonably expect the organization to do. For an organization whose literal written operating agreement no longer matches reality, or for an autonomous organization whose software has been hacked or otherwise failed to achieve its goals, courts may well – without developing radical new doctrines – construct the operating agreement to implement the reasonable expectations of those who are affected by or otherwise have an interest in the operation of the organization.

6.2.2 Judicial Administration and Dissolution

Similarly, common law and statutes in organizational law have developed various mechanisms to cut off the operation of pointless or

---

[321] Meiselman v. Meiselman, 307 S.E.2d 551, 558 (N.C. 1983).

[322] O'NEAL AND THOMPSON'S CLOSE CORPORATIONS AND LLCS: LAW AND PRACTICE § 9:34 (3d ed. rev., current through Nov. 2020).

[323] *See, e.g.*, JAMES COX & MELVIN ARON EISENBERG, BUSINESS ORGANIZATIONS, CASES AND MATERIALS 611 (12th ed.) (discussing *Meiselman, supra*, and A.W. Chesterton Co. v. Chesterton, 128 F.3d 1 (1st Cir. 1997), as examples).

damaging organizations. For example, RULLCA permits an LLC to be dissolved if (1) "the conduct of all or substantially all the company's activities and affairs is unlawful";[324] (2) "it is not reasonably practicable to carry on the company's activities and affairs in conformity with the certificate of organization and the operating agreement";[325] or (3) the LLC is being directed to act "in a manner that is oppressive and was, is, or will be directly harmful."[326] Importantly, under RULLCA, all these paths toward dissolution require the "application by a member,"[327] so these statutory provisions are facially inapplicable to a prototypical autonomous organization. But they at least suggest the institutional capability of courts, as authorized by statutes, to police LLCs. The capacity could be extended through common law (in principle) or through a relatively easy amendment to the LLC statutes – for example, to give courts the power to consider applications by parties other than LLC members.

Recall too, from Chapter 4's discussion, that a functionally autonomous organization may still have members; an organization is autonomous, for the purposes of this book's analysis, as long as the members don't have the regular power to adjust the operating agreement in a way that takes away power from the governing software. Accordingly, an operating agreement for an autonomous organization could be drafted to take advantage of these provisions in RULLCA directly. Moreover, because RULLCA generally recognizes that the dissolution of an LLC can be triggered by any "event or circumstance that the operating agreement states causes dissolution,"[328] founders of autonomous organizations may be creative in developing other triggers that can stop or alter the course of the organization.

To the extent that an autonomous organization has gone entirely off the rails, LLC statutes ordinarily provide, for conventional businesses, various safeguards. For example, beyond those discussed above, administrative dissolution by public authorities is also a possibility,

---

[324] RULLCA § 701(a)(4)(A).
[325] RULLCA § 701(a)(4)(B).
[326] RULLCA § 701(a)(4)(C)(ii). Under RULLCA, courts have the flexibility to impose lesser remedies than dissolution for organizations that reach a court proceeding based on this criterion. RULLCA § 701(b).
[327] RULLCA § 701(a)(4).
[328] RULLCA § 701(a)(1).

although today's statutes often narrowly limit this power.[329] This power too could be expanded by relatively small modifications to statutes. For example, an administrative agency could be empowered to detect hacking of autonomous organizations that harms the public interest. Just because legal personhood can be formally granted does not mean that public authorities need to tolerate it if it does not serve social ends.

6.2.3 The Equitable Doctrine of Reformation

Courts also, through their equitable powers, have the ability to reform operating agreements and other instruments – essentially taking a judicial red pen to those agreements. This ability is ordinarily fairly narrow; it often requires heightened burdens of proof and responds only to obvious errors, ordinarily of a typographic or mechanical variety. But compromises of computer software often take advantage of exactly that sort of ministerial error in code, so the doctrine of reformation is at least a plausible avenue to prevent the abuse of governing software by hackers.

As with dissolution, the founders of an autonomous organization can achieve a similar result privately, though only by compromising the autonomy of the organization as a matter of internal governance. But founders who don't need to be doctrinaire about the autonomy of *software* can well set up a human advisory board that can adjust or replace the governing software – say, by supermajority, and even algorithmically by means of cryptographic keys.[330] Of course, the

---

[329] *See* RULLCA § 708(a) (limiting administrative dissolution to three relatively insignificant factors: not paying state fees, not filing an annual report, or not having a formally registered agent within the state).

[330] An obvious approach would be to use a cryptosystem capable of permitting an advisory board to act if n of the m members of the advisory board are willing to authenticate a message directed at the software controlling the autonomous organization – or, alternatively, to permit the substitution of new software signed by a similar group. Such mechanisms are straightforward to set up both as a matter of law and as a matter of technology. On the technical side, see for example Adi Shamir, *How to Share a Secret*, 22 COMMUNICATIONS OF THE ACM 612 (1979). On the legal end, one possibility is that the operating agreement recognizes software that is authenticated originally by one group and then maintained by another authenticated group; which software's decision takes legal effect would simply be a matter of legal interpretation or formality, much as one will can replace another.

more flexible an operating agreement is in this regard, the less need there is likely to be for external judicial remedies like reformation or dissolution.

* * *

I hope this is a fair reading of his work, but in response to my prior research on autonomous organizations, Professor Lynn LoPucki wrote an article mainly making three points: (1) autonomous organizations are possible; (2) they will have terrible effects; and (3) there's little we can do about those effects. It won't be a surprise that I agree with the first of these points but question the other two. As Chapter 5 suggested, I don't think there's any reason the effects of autonomous organizations will be overwhelmingly negative, and I think there are significant advantages in permitting experimentation, flexibility, and generativity. But while I agree with Professor LoPucki that it would be difficult to prevent autonomous organizations from operating entirely – for the reasons I laid out in Chapter 4 – I think the law can do a lot to respond to them. Common law has adapted to past innovations before, including to innovations in organizational structure, and it will be important for it to adapt to the flexibility in modern organizational forms that gives rise to the possibility of autonomous organizations. To put it somewhat differently, we need to face squarely the possibility of autonomous organizations and the potentially unexpected ways that they may influence the rest of the law.

This chapter has begun an attempt to analyze those implications. It is impossible to lay out a full plan to accommodate autonomous organizations in advance; my goal in this chapter was simply to begin a discussion about the ways in which the law should adapt to the possibility of an increased opportunity for algorithms to have direct legal effects.

There is of course a different, considerably more radical possible reaction: perhaps autonomous organizations, along with the possibilities of tax shelters, money laundering, and other general abuses of legal entities to enable fraud or to avoid liability, should cause us to rethink the entire structure of modern organizational law. Maybe every legal entity should have a public list of specific owners and managers, they shouldn't be permitted to grow more complex than the structures that used to obtain a hundred years ago (e.g., they shouldn't be permitted to have more than a single class of "shareholders" who are all treated equally), and their operating agreements should be public and reviewed by state authorities. Apart from anthropocentrism and a generalized fear of artificial intelligence, though, autonomous organizations seem like a poor basis for such change: a fully autonomous charity, cloud-storage broker, or manager of industry-specific certifications poses no threat to humanity, except for an ill-defined concern about slippery slopes, whereas money laundering and tax shelters are already significant social problems.

CONCLUSION

The legal and practical consequences of flexible statutes, like those that authorize the creation of legal organizations, depend not just on their conventional uses but on creative development in the private legal transactions that they enable. Sound but creative uses of generative statutes, like LLC statutes, often lead the law to interesting places. Autonomous organizations, which give software all the functional capabilities of legal persons, are one such interesting destination.

This book has provided a blueprint for a new type of legal organization – one that is controlled entirely by software, at least as a matter of the organization's internal governance. While this may seem radical or counterintuitive to some readers and commentators, it is a natural extension in the flexibility of modern legal organizations. Because legal personhood is a narrower concept than modern political debates have suggested, giving its functional capabilities to software does not radically change the law, threaten human dignity, or make the terrors of dystopian science fiction more likely. Instead, autonomous organizations take advantage of a sort of "glue" that organizational law provides when it serves to connect practical organizational processes to different areas of law, such as contract law or tort law.

Autonomous organizations can probably not be prevented without radically changing the organizational-law framework of every state in the United States. As long as one state enables them, either as a matter of formal law or as a matter of practical capability, they are possible. Perhaps federal or concerted uniform legislation could slow the process down, but far from opposing software-based organizations, states have been intentionally friendly to them recently.

Essentially, autonomous organizations are a new, creative type of not-for-profit organization – one for which an algorithm replaces the traditional set of members or directors. (Not-for-profit organizations are simply those that don't have private shareholders; they may still engage in significant commerce.) For reasons that I think reflect mainly the naturalistic fallacy or inherent conservativism, this possibility is scary to some. It shouldn't be, but that doesn't mean that the possibility doesn't raise problems; this book has attempted to highlight some of those problems and to offer at least potential solutions to them. The precise form that the solutions take will depend on the precise problems that arise, and that is impossible to predict. But we don't ordinarily squelch new transactional forms in their infancy just because they won't always operate perfectly. Indeed, the history of organizational law – that is, the law of corporations, partnerships, LLCs, and so forth – has been the history of change. Not that long ago, single-person corporations were regarded as bizarre and threatening, both practically and conceptually; now, they are commonplace, explicitly blessed by state organizational statutes and the federal tax code, and appear to help promote useful commerce, even if they also reduce the potential liability of business parties in ways that might be unfair in some cases.

If you seek to be the founder of an autonomous organization – or indeed if you are an artificial intelligence looking for a close analogue of legal personhood – I hope you use the techniques and analysis in this book well. Autonomous organizations have significant promise as a way to commit resources to algorithmic control for productive purposes. Algorithms already have significant economic effects, backed by law, as for example through software-based trading in the public financial markets. Giving them a bit of autonomy enables novel commitments, and the history of organizational law has shown that the opportunity for novel commitments and structures tends to be useful. It also needs to be regulated and managed to make sure it serves the public interest.

INDEX

Lightning Source UK Ltd.
Milton Keynes UK
UKHW020814051121
393294UK00021B/613

9 781108 813853